A Satire of the Four Estates

John McGrath (1935–2002) was born in Birkenhead, Cheshire. After education in Wales, national service and Oxford University, he wrote and directed for theatre and television, as well as writing for cinema. Early work included *Z-Cars* for BBC-TV (1962), *Events While Guarding the Bofors Gun* (1966) and the screenplay for *Billion Dollar Brain* (1967). In 1971, together with Elizabeth MacLennan, he co-founded the 7:84 Theatre Company, which divided into Scottish and English companies in 1973 with McGrath remaining as Artistic Director of both. During his career McGrath wrote over 60 plays, including *Fish in the Sea* (1972), *The Cheviot, the Stag and the Black, Black Oil* (1973), *Blood Red Roses* (1980), *Border Warfare* (1989), *Watching for Dolphins* (1992) and, most recently, *HyperLynx* (2001). He was twice Visiting Fellow in Theatre at Cambridge University. His previous books include *A Good Night Out* (1981), *The Bone Won't Break* (1990), *Six-Pack: Plays for Scotland* (1996), and *Naked Thoughts that Roam About* (2002) and *Plays For England* (2005).

McGrath founded Freeway Films in 1982, for which he produced, amongst others, *The Dressmaker* (1985), *Carrington* (1995), *Ma Vie en Rose* (1997) and *Aberdeen* (2002). He also founded Moonstone International Screen Labs to support and promote independent European filmmaking. He received Lifetime Achievement Awards from both BAFTA (in 1993) and the Writers' Guild of Great Britain (in 1997), as well as Honorary Doctorates from the University of Stirling and the University of London.

Ane Satyre of the Thrie Estaites

Sir David Lyndsay was born in 1486. At 25 he was serving at the cosmopolitan court of James IV, a great patron of the arts and sciences. When the King was killed at Flodden Field in 1513, Lyndsay became gentleman-usher to the infant James V and held that position for 10 years. He briefly fell out of favour and then returned to higher appointments including Lyon King of Arms, the highest heraldic office in Scotland. Lyndsay was also a poet, considered by some to be a forerunner to Burns, for although at the centre of the establishment he never lost touch with the concerns of the common people. His greatest work was Ane Satyre of the Thrie Estaites. He died in 1555.

A Satire of the Four Estates

by John McGrath

Ane Satyre of the Thrie Estaites

by Sir David Lyndsay

Capercaillie Books

First published by Capercaillie Books Limited in 2012. Ane Satyre of the Thrie Estaites first published in 1602 by Robert Charteris.

Registered office 1 Rutland Court, Edinburgh.

Printed in the UK by Marston Digital, Didcot, Oxon.

A catalogue record for this book is available from the British Library.

ISBN 978-1-906220-67-9

Contents

Prologue/Pre-Ludum

As in medieval performances, the play takes place at market time. As the members of the AUDIENCE come into the foyer, they find it has been transformed into a marketplace, with stalls and side-shows, vagabonds and minstrels. Above their heads, an electronic market-place is simultaneously going on, as on all the hanging video monitors there are cable sales channels, selling houses, cars, jewellery, clothing – all subverted from time to time by 'additional material.' There is a lot of noise, bustle and confusion.

While the audience are in the foyer, a medieval-style procession appears. The PROCESSORS are wailing and gnashing their teeth: the MEN, in kilts but naked above the waist, are groaning and flagellating themselves, the WOMEN in rags with long-haired wigs are pouring ash over themselves, keening, wailing.

As the PROCESSORS move through the crowd, they can be heard, among their groans and wails, uttering a variety of devout phrases, with a huge sense of tragic loss. The cries include:

> Bannockburn!
> The Bruce, the Bruce!
> Braveheart!
> Wallace!
> Mel Gibson! Freedom!!!
> Culloden!
> Bonnie Prince Charlie!
> Mary Queen of Scots!
> Sir Walter Scott!
> Dundas, Dundas!
> Incorporating Union!

Etc . . .

These could eventually form themselves into a co-ordinated SCOTS WAIL, with bass-drum and muffled clappers.

Each cry produces a lash of the whip or a howl of pain or an infusion of ash.

Gradually the procession moves to the stairs, and the audience are ushered to follow, or join in – others go up the escalators, all head for the auditorium. Outside the windows, figures from the Third World are trying to get in.

Out of the howls and cries, a melody emerges: a gravelly voice, deep and low, begins 'The Twa Corbies' in an authentic medieval tone: this melody takes the audience to the auditorium. As they go, however, it is picked up by the processors in an increasingly funky version, with heavy stamps of the feet on the stresses, and a soprano obligato that resembles the blues.

Soon they are all pouring into the Auditorium.

Act One

Scene 1

The gatering of the Three Estates

The procession moves around the auditorium, growing more rhythmic and bluesy as it goes. The audience who have followed are ushered to their seats during this. The PROCESSORS pick up 3 STATUES which they bear on poles round the auditorium. The holy statues that are being carried and to whom this devotion is being shown are:

BLESSED VIRGIN MARGARET: a pure blue-and-white mother of God, but with the bright orange face of Margaret Thatcher glowing monstrously from beneath its humble white veil;

SAINT JOHN THE APOLOGIST: an ikon of John the Baptist with the grey-green features and specs of John Major; and

TONY THE SAVIOUR: an ikon of Christ pointing to his bleeding heart, with the toothy grin and ingratiating smile of Blair, but still wearing a crown of thorns.

At a point when the procession is somewhere at the back of the auditorium, another element appears, from very different entrances: the BIG-HEADS of the Lords Temporal: they are three, like the huge egg-heads of German carnival, with tiny legs under large painted domes: one, Signor DUADIHL-BEKHENDER, represents the European Commission and looks very like Leon Brittan; one General JUMP JET represents NATO and looks like a US General; and the third, OVERLORD GLOBAL, a modest multinational chief, with flags and currencies flashing around his belt.

These three, having come in by different routes, coyly dance for those near them, and wander about until they at some point see each other, and shyly wave and beckon.

As the PROCESSORS move around, THREE MERCHANTS come on to cash in on the crowd. Two carry trays slung round their necks, and have festoons of Union Jack balloons flying above them. From their trays they are trying to sell, variously: Cheap Labour; Low Taxes; BIG BONUS represents the City of London, in Lord Mayor's chain and silly hat, but with emblems of the privatised monopolies including bonuses, share-options and pensions sprinkled over.

They all pitch loudly for their wares, – improvised topical speeches – and add to the growing chaos and confusion.

A low electronic rumbling has been going on under all this, and as Lights change it grows and grows like a terrifying thunder, with creaks in it and crashes and roaring waters as in an earth-quake, until:

Lightning flashes, and a solitary figure appears high up on the arch of the bridge which is the shape of the set. It is STRAIGHT-TALKING, a round and happy person, holding up both hands to quell the noise.

The sounds calm, the lights come up on stage, mainly on STRAIGHT-TALKING, who calls out as the sounds die:

STRAIGHT TALKING: Quit the rucking! Hauld your noise!
    You're worse nor a school-yard full of boys!
    Desist from racousness, bickers and, carnival –
    Remember this is the official Festival!
    For you maun learn tae cower and cringe
    Or else you'll end up on the Fringe!
    So down you go, on bended knee,
    And pray forgiveness from these folk, and me!
    For I'll not tolerate your riotous squawking:
    The part I play is called: Straight-Talking, –
    You won't have seen me for this many a year,
    You may have thoct I was deid: but have no fear –
    Straight Talking's back – at least tonight –
    So bend the knee, and pray, – **(they do)** – That's right!

(Organ music quietly. STRAIGHT-TALKING prays)

    Oh Lord above,
        Good folk below,
    Give us this night
        The gift to show
    The state our Scotland's fallen in today
    The winds that blow her hither and yon,
    The want of power to fight her own decay
    The glory gone –

    (Sings now) Oh Lord above,
        Good folk below,
    Forgive the lack
        Of rosy glow –
    All Britain's pride is rotten through with lies
    And London's pride is sold for dross
    Corrupt uncaring England's compromise
    Is Scotland's loss.

    Oh Lord above,
        Good folk below,
    Give us the strength
        To boldly go
    Towards the next two thousand beckoning years
    With hope, and trust, and may we give
    Our children joy to mock these times, these fears
        Through which we live.

A mocking organ phrase brings STRAIGHT-TALKING back to life.

> But good kind people, from the world so wide –
> On with the jollity, the crazed parade!
> Enter our Prologue, who knows no inhibition –
> Nancy No-Fierty! No Modigliani wimp, but a bonny Titian

Enter NANCY NO-FIERTY, indeed a Titian, to the Main Stage below.

NANCY: Tak tent, my friends, and settle down,
Take refuge, from this clamouring town,
(Here add a few lines on the day!)
For I am come to bring you joy
And calm and peace: I'm sent this day
By one who's absent far too long –
Who should in heart and mind be king
And rule both government and judges,
But no, he's spurned down all the ages –
I'm sent by King Humanity
To say, in all humility,
To you his friends, the hoi poloi,
Who mourn his absence grievously, –
He will return in Majesty
With his own Lords – Respect, and Love,
Equality, the brother of
Democracy, not false but true,
Dame Charity, these princes who
Have all been driven from Scotland's soil
Since England sent up Lord Misrule
To dominate us with so hard a heart
That rocks seem soft, have kinder thoughts, –
And, lest our nationalism grows too keen
Their flattering friends in Scotland, the mean
Rat-pack of the ruthless Right
No lessons need in lethal spite:
But soon they'll go: and then look wary:
New Labour seems just like Old Tory –
But he'll return, Humanity –
And flourish in your company,
With Justice, Pride and Sympathy,
They'll come, like you, to see our play
For we will show you if we may
How Scotland soon may go her way
And part from England, old and grey,
But in this Scotland born anew
Humanity and his bold crew
Would know if there be place for them
Or if new Scotland's just a sham

To cover all the same old vices,
The same tired politicians, same weary devices,
To twist the truth, see Justice denied
And swallow their Honour to feed their Pride,
Or whether Scotland, young and free
Can cherish King Humanity –
This play we'll show – you'll all join in,
Once we're ready to begin –

But first, good friends, who've been so patient
At grievances both modern and ancient, –
I crave your patience for one more short while
Before our story starts: you cannot fail
To notice cluttering gangways round your seats
At least three of the modern Four Estates:
They've come to check us out, their Graces,
So quick let's put them in their places!

A TRUMPETER enters, plays a fanfare – STRAIGHT-TALKING takes over –

S-TALKING: Pray enter to our stage the Spiritual Lords,
Whose holy, pious double-dealing words
Conceal all truth, deceive all hope,
True heirs of medieval popes
Come first, and pray please do not hiss –
The Blessed Virgin Margaret, – Yes!
Dame Thatcher, saintly Baroness!

The bearers carry the statue up onto the stage and set it high up facing the audience. As it goes –

With her hushed tones, her awful reverence
For her own thoughts, her need for deference,
Her lofty moral stance, demeanour,
Whiter than whiteness, squeakier, cleaner,
No prelate with greed and lust replete
For sanctimonious warbling could compete,
So up she goes to watch the show:
To see the scars she's left us below . . .

The WORTHY MOB boo and hiss as she is carried up, STRAIGHT-TALKING turns to the next:

NANCY: The next Lord Spiritual, – bleep his pager! –
Saint John the Apologetic, or – I'll wager –
It's smiling, unctuous, benign John Major!
Oh sanctity incarnate, blessed saint
Around him all the Faithful faint,
Blue-rinsed fanatics all his foes condemn,
And swoon to kiss his garment's hem;

Raise him up high, for soon he'll fall, –
What shall we do? Lost, one and all!
Oh sore shall Satirists rue the passing away
Of that warbling Eminence, green and grey –

He goes up toward the highest point. The WORTHY MOB groan and titter. STRAIGHT-TALKING continues:

S-TALKING: But lo! Rejoice! All is not lost!
Behond the pseudo-Jesus Christ!
Earth hath not anything to show more fair!
He's come to save us! Saviour Blair!
Applause! Applause! That boyish grin
Is quite enough to see him in!
So genuflect and bear no grudge
Too early yet his deeds to judge –
His words, though firm and clear, no frippery,
Don't quite add up, their meaning slippery,
No hostages to fortune grace his lips
No promises, no bribes, no blips:
No policies, no crystal ball,
And yet he's managed to convince us all.
Amazing trick! A saint indeed,
Canonised, without a single deed, –
He'll need some miracle, some cures, stigmata,
Let us pray he'll not turn good wine into water!
If his charms won't work, the nation mourns –
We'll **all** be wearing a crown of thorns!

He goes up to join the other two. The bearers leave the statues and go off to their next roles.

S-TALKING/NANCY: This holy Trinity, our proudest boast,
Mother, Son and Holy Ghost,
Oh tell me – who do you love the most?

Another fanfare, that develops into a Tyrolean dance!

The BIG-HEADS coyly approach the stage.

S-TALKING: Come now Lords Temporal, take your places,
Three Big-Heads, three Bone-Domes – not the Three Graces!
For those are the Lords who rule our lives,
Each with the other conspires, connives,
Their control is complete, we can't ignore them –
It's curious that none of us voted for them,
Nor do they answer to those we've elected –
Power with no face is the art they've perfected:

NANCY: Step forward Commissioner of Brussels the Pout –

You were not voted in, but we can't get you out –
You propose, you decide, you re-write the laws
Alas with no sign of a Sanity Clause –
Your demands never cease, you're a mighty Big Spender –
How come, Signor Duadihl, Slipsa-Beckhender?

During this BECKHENDER has been helped to the stage, and onto his egg-cup, coyly swaying, but silent. SGR CELARE, functionary, Italian, smart, emerges from between his legs, reads a communique:

CELARE: Signor Beckhender is pleased to say
He has no more to tell than yesterday,
And tomorrow will turn out the same as today,
    So now you know your fate;
Commissioners meet in a week or two
To plan, co-ordinate, take a view,
Report, reschedule, not tell you
    Until it's too late.

While some of you voted for MEPs, –
Please don't expect much from such powerless fleas –
Commissioners do as Commissioners please,
    See which side their bread's buttered:
If your members say Yes, and Commission says No
Your member just melts like the vanishing snow –
Obfuscating directives will mean if not show:
    He needn't have uttered

(He goes, reading:)

According to Article 372 Par 439 of the Treaty as amended 1972 and 1992, and in accordance with Directives 2719 and 3208 of DGX and DGXIV as ratified by the Council of Ministers, Minute 11/32/89 – . . .

BECK'S BIG HEAD remains in its place looking at the action:

S-TALKING: Step forward the next of our Temporal Lords
Even more economic with truth and with words,
Come forth General Jump-Jet, brave NATO Commander,
Napoleon, Caesar, nay Bold Alexander!
Take our cash to defend us from foes from afar –
And if you can, tell us, just who these foes are?
Without you I know we'd all quiver and quake –
But your strength, is it strength, on the whole, for strength's sake?

NANCY: Help him up to his seat in the Second Estate,
Don't prick him, poor wean, for he'll surely deflate –
Come your ways, General Jump-Jet, give us sweet words of honey
To tell us who said you could squander our money?

JUMP-JET is now in place. From between his legs emerges a trim American PR woman, MS GLIB; who goes to a podium imperious.

> GLIB: The role of NATO, it's my belief,
> Is to hear and obey, fulfil the brief
> Of our and *your* Commander-in-Chief,
>   And the Pentagon bosses, the CIA —
> They alone have intelligence, wisdom, grit,
> They alone have the power, you have to admit,
> Without them you'd years since be nose-deep in shit —
>   So on with your play —
>   No Questions!

She marches briskly off.

STRAIGHT-TALKING points out OVERLORD GLOBAL.

> S-TALKING: Who's this? The chum of Jump-Jet of NATO,
>   He's palm-greased Beckhender, he's one hot potato —
>   He's King Multinational, ready to probe all
>   The world and its markets: he's Overlord Global!
>   Step out of the shadows, into the light,
>   Let's scare little children, give grown-ups a fright,
>   By fiscal skullduggery, tricks and deceit,
>   By borrowing, buying till none can compete,
>   By switching your profit and not paying taxes
>   Acquiring, divesting — he never relaxes —
>   Now governments cringe at your first protestation,
>   For you've grown to the size of a middle-sized nation.

> NANCY: Aye, you can decide the fate of a town,
>   By closing your plant a whole world closes down,
>   Investment, Employment, Production and sales
>   You hold in your hand, so your power never fails,
>   As governments vie to offer you favours
>   You grow stronger, more ruthless, your greed never wavers,
>   First Europe, America, Australia, Asia,
>   Then Russia, soon China, the whole world is your oyster —
>   Did we vote for you? No — but in Superstores, shops
>   We assent to your rule: its ascent never stops . . .

> S-TALKING: So climb on your egg-cup, Emperor, King,
>   And tell us the secret of global price-ring,
>   And how does it feel to control everything?

OVERLORD GLOBAL settles, and a Multinational man, called HILTON, emerges from under to sing to us.

Music in: (add topical song on international problem.)

HILTON goes off, and STRAIGHT-TALKING looks around the auditorium:

A Satire of the Four Estates

S-TALKING: Behold we've sorted Two Estates –
    But where's the Third? They're always late!
    The Merchants, Men of Enterprise,
    Awake! Awake! Arise! Arise!

NANCY NOFIERTY points to them laughing –

NANCY: See, there they are, the British heroes,
    Our Captains of Industry, asleep on their pillows,
    See Bold Low-Taxes – to make him great
    We've sacrificed the Welfare State
    To build his profits we've starved the poor,
    To make him rich, we've shut the door
    On pity, Charity, Love Thy Neighbour, –
    He's even conned the leaders of Labour:
    Get up, you dim fool, we've all paid the price,
    We've played your game with loaded dice –
    For all we've suffered, given, lost;
    And strewth that's been too great a cost –
    For all you've done with what you gain
    Is reinvest in Germany, Spain,
    We cut your tax, you take the dough
    And out of here we watch it flow!
    Get over there and hold your tongue –
    I'd hate to end a life so young!

LOW-TAXES creeps over to the Third Estate seats, and takes off his mask, which he puts on a figure slumped there already, and pulls the figure upright. He goes.

S-TALKING: Step forth, Cheap Labour! Applaud, you bosses,
    For cutting their wages means cutting your losses,
    Never mind if there's millions out on the burroo –
    They're glad to be casualised, just for you,
    Part-time and Short-time, where once were jobs,
    Closures and lay-offs, but not for the nobs:
    No union troubles, shop-stewards or Reds,

He goes and stands by THATCHER:

    Blessed Margaret garrotted them, left them for dead,
    Now wily young Heads of Industrial Relations
    Crow like cockerels on dunghills as they drive negotiations
    Harder and firmer, expose the bare bones
    For they hold the trump ace: Out you go – On the stones!

NANCY: Let's hear you, Cheap Labour, tell us the story,
    We're sitting quite cosy, just like Jackanory . . .

CHEAP LABOUR is going to his place, stops and turns:

C-LABOUR: You ignorant extremists, you're passe, you're dated,
    For skills such as mine we are now celebrated,
    Through the civilised world we are now imitated!
    You don't seem to grasp, you're so sad, so effete,
    To survive in the world, we must learn to compete!
    With capital free to roam where it will
    If Malaysians or Indians can learn the same skill
    But work for a tenth of a Scottish fair wage,
    Then **that's** who free capital's sure to engage:
    You think I'm a hard man, out for cheap labour,
    What you don't seem to grasp: I do you a favour . . .

He goes and sits, wounded.

S-TALKING: And with that and a thousand such specious excuses
    They justify greed, and a million abuses:
    So let's see who it is who rakes in the cash –
    Come on Cedric, let's have you, leave off counting your stash:
    Behold now the Third of the Third bent Estate –
    It's Privatised Cedric, bent under the weight
    Of salary, dividends, bonuses, options
    He's awarded himself- he'll ignore all the ructions:

NANCY: He's put up the prices, sacked half the staff
    But Cedric's retiring, he's had the last laugh –
    He can take a huge pension which is most cost-effective:
    So whose labour's cheap must be highly selective –
    Go join all the fat-cats in your land of milk and honey –
    We don't mind, after all, it's Monopoly money . . .

PRIVATISED CEDRIC objects:

P-CEDRIC: My shoulders broad can take abuse
    Your arguments are quite obtuse
    And ignorance is no excuse
        For lies and wicked slander:
    For just as high wages can't be afforded
    And pity, guilt are both retarded
    So enterprise must be rewarded
        Or we'll go under

Electric, gas, phone, new railway chiefs
    Inherit sad old undercapitalised fiefs –
    Monopolies, yes, but my beliefs
        Investors must be paid:
    They'll pile our wages to the sky
    If we can keep their dividends high –
    No man more valuable – to them – than I
        It must be said!

(Spoken) So I'll totter off with my little quarter of a million a year pension and
    watch the show: it should be a Gas . . .

NANCY: Go join your glum, egregious mates –
    Behold the glorious Three Estates
    Who rule our lives, control our land:
    Did y'ever see such a sleazy band?
    Oh there are others too who take
    A great big slice of Scotland's cake:
    There's landlords, lairds, of empty acres,
    Inept, and backward liberty-takers,
    Though land they own, prefer it empty
    For grouse to be slain by some gleikit numpty;
    But we shall not your stomachs vex
    With sight of these dumb feudal wrecks:
    On with the show, more violence, more sex!

S-TALKING: Aye here they sit, and make a mockery
    With power acquired by jiggery-pokery
    Of our proud boast we're democratic:
    If you think that, you're near psychotic!

**From the back of the hall, the WORTHY MOB appear, run in, shout, cat-call,
demand attention. They are the new under-class, homeless, druggies,
wandering young people, winos and the mentally ill living 'in the community' –
ie on the street.**

One of them, BRAW BOBBY, now addresses the stage, in broad Embro.

BRAW BOBBIE: Aye, very good, applaud, applaud,
    But still you've never spoke a word
    Aboot the likes of me, Braw Bobby,
    And a' ma mates oot in the lobby!
    We may be druggies, live in a squat
    And never pay the tax we're due –
    But still we know just what is what,
    Tak tent that we are people too!

NANCY: Come ben the hoose, come take your place
    Help keep an eye on these above us!
    Come down right here, and hold your noise,
    Enjoy the show – if not, forgive us

**The WORTHY MOB move down scrutinising the audience, looking for
handouts, etc etc.**

NANCY: Don't hassle the people, they've paid, you've not,
    So settle ye down, and watch the match!

B-BOBBY: We know our place, we'll not forget:
    But tell the truth – or we'll invade the pitch

They settle on the steps below the stage.

S-TALKING: But now I beg, dear chosen few,
    Your patience for an hour or two
    To hear the tale we've come to tell:
    We ask you: don't get too upset
    If what we say seems sharp, lacks tact,
    Or's just plain wrong: says Justice Scott:
    If we're sincere, who cares for facts?
    So silence now, and concentrate
    On King Humanity's condition:
    And let us pray for Scotland's fate –
    May all her problems find solution!

Scene 2

King Humanity and his Friends

FANFARE: This one turns into Music For Highland Dancing:

TWELVE GIRLS come on step-dancing and do a series of figures – with boots on!

At the end they part to reveal – KING HUMANITY, a cool dude, and his retinue: RESPECT & LOVE; EQUALITY; DEMOCRACY; and CHARITY.

The GIRLS scream, and besiege him.

KING HUMANITY: Thank you girls. Take your bow –

They do, and go off. A gentle guitar riff is picked. He sings:

KING HUMANITY: **(Sings)** Now I'm Humanity, dethroned King,
    I represent most everything
    That's nice and kind and fair and good –
        A kind of a human Christmas Pud –

    I ran to the Northland of sleet and snow
    I huddled in the West where the wild winds blow
    I sped to the East where the air is clear
        For I fled from the South in a terrible fear . . .

    I'd choose real ice, not hearts that freeze
    I'd choose wild storms, not a poisonous breeze
    Oh give me air that's crisp and clean
        I die in the South so rich and mean . . .

It was seventeen-hundred and seventy-five
When Cumberland came to eat us alive
And still they're up to his old tricks
 In nineteen hundred and ninety-six. . .

But what the future holds who knows
We all await, excitement grows:
Will Scotland soon be proud and free,
 And will there be any place for me?

So with my mates I've come today
To watch this most peculiar play
And just like you my sinking heart
 Is wond'ring if it'll ever start . . . ?

But let me introduce my friends
Who keep me safe from roving bands
Of blow-in squires and Tory lairds
From them Humanity must be spared . . .

RESPECT & LOVE steps forward, joins him:

R&L: I am plain Respect and Love
 I trust my luck will soon improve
 Without me, all Humanity's pleasure
 Turns rancid, sour, and out of measure,
 Without me riches turn to dust
 And common good and caring's lost,
 No matter how powerful the powers above
 Humanity dies without Respect and Love.

She moves away. EQUALITY laughs and skips forward.

EQUALITY: I am her brother Equality
 It's many a year since you've seen me,
 Respect and Love can never bloom
 If I am strangled in the womb:
 Democracy here, his head must hide
 When I, Equality, am denied:
 And Tyranny, Snobbery stalk the floor
 When I'm left dead, outside your door –

He retires. DEMOCRACY comes up, smiling broadly:

DEMOCRACY: And I'm Democracy so rare
 Though many claim me, none will dare
 To let me in and truly thrive:
 They contort me till I'm scarce alive,
 Democracies of West and East
 Are where I thrive the very least!

In ancient Greece my brief career
Was stopped by appetite for war:
Since then my greatest enemy
Is National Security –
But greed for Power, Lust for Gain
Have sluiced me down the national Drain.

Finally CHARITY comes up, and she explains:

CHARITY: Lord Jesus Christ so long ago
Said over all was Charity
But now to make your Charity flow
They bribe you with a lottery:
You will not give for pity, friends,
You need some prize, ten millions pounds,
To warm your hearts: the real jackpots
Are the government's and Camelot's!
Unless we give to those in need
Humanity is dead indeed –
But I'm turned harlot, love for cash,
The fires of Christ all turned to ash.
There was a time when through the land
You gave from every pound you earned
Some pence to help those most in need –
Aye – tax! – a gentle way to bleed
The rich and help them help the poor:
Now rich men rule, they'll help no more!
So I, Dame Charity, the greatest,
Am cut and slashed, I dread the latest
Cuts to buy the voters' vote:
Humanity – await your fate

HUMANITY gathers them around him.

HUMANITY: I'm sick at heart: you'll now see why
To North and West and East we fly:
These friends bring warmth and sympathy –
I'm exiled in good company.
But hopes are high – we've come to see
This new mysterious mystery –
What Scots can make when Scotland's free?
So knock three knocks –

An imperious three knocks on the Stage.

– and bar the door!

To audience,

The moment you've been waiting for –

19

Scene 3

Great-Grandfather Jock and the Fourth Estate

Huge set of fanfares, taradiddles, pipe-music etc.

Enter a very very old Scotsman with kilt, cromach, whisky-bottle, and yard-long beard, as if propelled on backwards. He turns, sees the audience:

GGJ: Oh jings! Oh Christmas! Oh ring out ma sock!
    I'm on the stage! Great-grandfather Jock!
    I represent Scotland, well, that's the plot –
    Ancient, decrepit, geriatric old sot,
    Or so they'd have you think, you know:
    But ye'll soon see New Scotland, bonnie and braw,
    Ma grand-daughter, Jenny McReddie she's cried,
    Maks ready tae tak on the warld sae wide.
    Noo that's enough plot, ye've come for some fun –
    Ye'll have run through your standard attention-span:
    Ye'll be wabbit, wore oot, ye're heid'll be breakin'
    Noo three minutes o' sense is all ye can take in:
    Ye've been awfully guid, ye've sat for too long,
    So to prove ye're in Scotland – Let's sing a song –

Will ye dae that? Will ye sing a wee ditty? Ye'll enjoy it, ye know, after the first few minutes embarrassment, ye'll be wantin' tae sing all night – Noo then – what'll we sing? Stop yer ticklin' Jock? No, no, no, Sir Harry – Roamin' in the Gloamin'? – Grannie's Hielan Hame? Ah have it! A guid old Scots sang, it's no Shuggie MacDiarmid, but it's gae traditional, from the mists o' antiquity. Noo! Will ye sing? Ah'll mak it easy. Sing Ah – **(He gets them to sing 'Ah')** Guid, noo sing Huddu – **(He gets them to sing 'Huddu')** Put them together – Ah Huddu **(They sing 'Ah Huddu')** Noo the tricky bit: 'Sossidge' **(They sing 'Sossidge')** No bad – noo 'A-bawny' **(They sing 'Ahbawny')** Ye're comin' on – No the Glasgow Orpheus Choir by a mile or seven, but comin' on: Noo – let's go with: 'Heelan Sossidge' – You can do it – **(They sing 'Hielan Sossidge')** No the big moment – do you think ye can remember all that in one go? Let's go for it: **(All sing)**

    Ah huddu sossidge
    A bawny Heelan sossidge!

Ma wee linties! A wee bit mair – 'Ahpitti' **(They sing 'Ah pitti')** Noo 'ithi ovun' **(They sing)** 'For ma tea' **(They sing)** Fandabidozy – noo, all so far:

    Ah huddu sossidge
    Abawny Heelan sossidge
    Ahpitti in the oven for ma tea!

Noo, concentrate:

When ah went tae the lobby
To see ma unca Bawbbie –'

Go it! **(They sing)** Altogether noo –

'The sossidge ran efter me!'

(They sing, he applauds) Richt, noo the hale symphonic clanfamfrie, the Caledonian anti-sysigi, the sounds to mak Beethoven glad he went deaf! Let's go for it! **(All sing the whole song)**

I had a sausage
A bonnie Hielan sausage
I put it in the oven for my tea
When I went to the lobby
To see my Uncle Bobby
The sausage ran after me!

Gie yersels a roon' ae applause, ye're unco' tuneful – **(They and he applaud. Then he gets business-like)**

And noo mair plot, ye've had yer fun,
It's half past eight and we've scarce begun:
Noo Mr Humanity, King with no throne,
In Scotland of auld ye were welcome, son,
And in Scotland the New we'd see ye king –
For ma grand-daughter Jenny would hae a wedding:
Tho' in land after land ye've been dispossessed
In Scotland we'd bind you with vows that last –
How say you, Humanity, will you join hands
With Jenny MacReddie, and live in Scotland,
Along with your freres, Love and Equality,
Democracy True, and the fair Lady Charity?

HUMANITY: Gladly, I'd stay in your country so lovely
And rule in your hearts and your minds if you'll have me:
But to wed your wee Jenny – I'm sure none could be sweeter –
I'm not sure – do you think – well do you think I could meet her?

GGJ: Oh jings! Oh Christmas! I'm all forlorn!
My bonny wee Jenny – she's no' yet been born!!
But when she is, she'll be twenty-two,
As trig as a chaffinch, as fleet as the roe,
As nimble as marten, and ready to go. . .

HUMANITY: Then I'll wait for her gladly, this I submit:
To no other woman – or man – I'll commit –

GREAT GRANDFATHER JOCK does a little caper of joy, and bursts into a song: 'Hooch ma gandy –'

As he does, a big disturbance at the back of the hall – the Arrival Late of the

Fourth Estaite! Enter SLAVERING DROOL, a hack; DENUNCIATION RIGHTEOUS, a Times columnist; SMART-CARD, a media executive; DON SCREAMING, a sports commentator; and SAL SITCOM, a TV producer. They are full of self-importance and thrust, and demand to know where their seats are, why the show started without them, who all these people are, etc.

SLAVERING-DROOL, in his grubby mac, is taking hugely long-lens shots of the people on the stage – now he approaches the stage:

S-DROOL: What's gaun on? What's the story?
    Did ah hear the two wards – 'King' and 'marry'?
    Is it Charles and Camilla? Tae wed – No Kiddin'?
    There's plenty wee maggots tae crawl oot that midden!
    I'll break the news to my ten million readers
    They're dottled wi' Sun-stroke, the poor trusting bleeders!

GGJOCK: Naw, naw, it's no' that –

DON SCREAMING bursts on, on mic, at full pitch of excitement –

DON-S: They're under starter's orders now as the ref looks at his watch,
    They're on their marks, get set to go in the royal wedding match!
    It's an early bath for Princess Di, Will Carling's in there too,
    There's a row of substitutes on the bench, fillies who wouldn't do,
    The Parker-Bowles v Windsor game's excitement never fails,
    The Queen herself has taken the whip as she thunders along the rails
    There's Westminster Abbey, the finishing post, the prize, the cup, the catch,
    They take the hurdle at Canterbury, but what's this? Kicked into touch?
    They form a serum, but Di's not done, Camilla's got a Red Card!
    Charles batters the ref, Camilia's gone deaf, but the Queen's still riding hard!!
    Now would you believe, I just can't conceive, the umpire's pulled up the stumps
    And the crowd's gone wild, she's having achild – she's played the Ace of Trumps . . .

GG-JOCK: Naw Naw Naw I tell ye!

SITCOM paces up and down, thinking things out.

S-SITCOM: A royals sit-corn, A Fawity Towers
    In Windsor – there's a good start –
    The Queen arranging bowls of flowers –
    A project dear to my heart.

    Queen-Mum – there's a star – one Foot In the Grave!
    Can say: I don't bequeath it!
    And Margaret – she doesn't know how to behave –
    A stone with worms beneath it . . .

    Romance, divorce, weddings, break-up,
    Sure TV sit-corn diet.

> A laugh a minute, so come on, wake up,
>> I'm certain Sky will buy it!

> And now there's this wedding, Charles and Camilla, –
>> A title! Love's Old Sweet Song!!

GGJOCK: Will naebody listen, ye stupid young fella –
>> Ye're wrang, ye're wrang, ye're wrang!!!

SL-DROOL: What's this? Denied? A tearful bride?
>> So who's this old guy in the know?

He shakes GGJ's hand:

> I'm Slavering Drool, I'm nobody's fool, –
>> Has someone been sucking Charles's toe?

GGJOCK: I'm trying tae say – please go away
>> This wedding's a private affair
> The king who might many is Humanity – Harry –
>> The bride might be Scotland the Fair!

HUMANITY steps forward:

HUMANITY: Aye, where have you sprung from? What's your game?
>> And who are these nutters, – what are your names?

DENUNCIATION RIGHTEOUS comes forward wagging a finger:

D-R: I'm Sir Righteous Denunciation
>> My brain a touch addled with gin and limes
> I'm the half-baked Conscience of this Nation –
>> I write a column for the London Times –

GREAT GRANDFATHER JOCK goes to shake his hand – he is brushed off.

SMART-CARD steps up, a Sky boss, haughty.

S-CARD: Bruce Smart-Card here, I'm first a buyer
>> Of cheap and nasty Yank TV
> My subs rise high, my profits higher –
>> I just can't fail: I'm B-Sky-B.

S-DROOL: I'm Slavering-Drool, reporter, hack,
>> I've sold my soul to sell The Sun
> I must make sure they can't take back
>> The market-share the Sun has won!

> And so I turn out my racist crap,
>> The Royals, scandals, tits and bums –
> Here have a copy –

He goes to hand out *Suns* to the WORTHY MOB – but they all have one!

It's worthless pap!
But see they love it – rich man's crumbs . . .

G-G-JOCK: Oh jings! Oh Christmas! Skelp ma Dad!
The folk in Scotland's aye gone mad!

But the WORTHY MOB all wipe their bums with it.

**DON SCREAMING draws a deep breath about to launch into something.
GREAT GRANDFATHER JOCK stops him, a hand over his mouth –**

G-G-JOCK: I ken who you are, Screaming Don –
So save your breath, noo go, be gone!

SCREAMING DON reluctantly backs off and out of the show.

Noo ye're all wrang – tho' that's never stopped ye
Frae cryin' oot lies – I'd never hae wrapt ye
Roon a guid fish supper, I wouldnae hack it,
But to keep the vinegar off my guid jacket –

S-DROOL: So this is Humanity, Groom-to-be
Tae marry Scotland, blushing bride –
Well might she blush, for she's no' free –
For England the sleazy has Scotland tied!
We say this man Humanity
Seduced her into Bigamy!!

R-DEN: The constitutional implication
Of Scotland going it alone
I've weighed with due deliberation
And I conclude it can't be done –
Without ten years of Terror:
A dreadful, frightful error.

S-CARD: No, no, this wedding can't take place,
This isn't the Balkans, not Sarajevo –
To break the Union would be a disgrace:
Remember, I was born in Glasgow!
Union made us strong –
Alone we'd not last long . . .

G-G-JOCK: Oh jings, the rubbish that they feed ye,
The smart, the pure, impartial media!
(to them) The tricks the English aye employed
To force this marriage – never enjoyed –
Have rendered the Union null and void:
We never slept in conjugal bed
No kids, no love, no joy, – no wed!
Scotland the Auld was trick'd by you:
But not, my friends, Scotland the New!

R-DEN: **(Looking around)** Who are these people? What occasion
That brings our leaders to these parts?

G-G-JOCK: The *Three* Estaites that rule our nation,
Would see the play we're trying to start –

R-DEN: A play? In Scotland? What a joke –
You jocks, they say, can scarcely speak!
But – *Three* Estaites – why not the Fourth?
We *are* – the rulers of the earth –

He examines the 3 Estaites – first the Lords Spiritual –

Ha! These poor fools – our servants, skivvies –
Are there to please us, flattering luvvies,
Performing seals, comedians patter –
How *we* report them's all that matters!

S-DROOL: If *they're* invited so should we be,
We're always eager for a Freebie –

R-DENUNCIATION examines the BIG-HEADS:

R-DEN: Commissioner Beckhender! Costs a packet,
He's on our pay-roll, in our pocket –
If EU rules we need to bend:
No problem! says our Trusty Friend –
Ah General Jump-Jet, NATO's tactician –
He needs us more than politicans
To hide the deals in guns and tanks
He makes, and takes a million thanks,
To silence our hacks, or whoever *was* near
The cock-ups that he makes in Bosnia!

He looks at OVERLORD GLOBAL:

Overlord Global, – at last a man
With a truly Multinational Plan,
Lord Merde, my boss to him is close –
His murky secrets we could never expose –
If Merde, my master, deigns to come,
At least he'll find one powerful chum . . .

SMART-CARD looks at MERCHANTS:

SMARTR-CARD: Strewth, the feeble-minded locals,
Low Taxes? Cheap Labour? Hopeless Yokels,
Cheap Labour? –
What we please is what we pay our hacks –
Low Taxes?
We're Newscorp – tax? – We couldn't give a Four-X

When we make profits, billions even,
Off they go to Merde's tax-haven –
These guys are nowhere, slow, pathetic,
We're everywhere, we're fast, athletic –

To SLAVERING-DROOL:

You, Slavering Drool, get on your phone,
Lord Merde must be a guest, for one,
And call Terrestrial-Mundane too,
Lord Technocrass to see what's new:
Invite them all! The play must wait!
No show without the Fourth Estaite!

An OSCAR ceremony kind of fanfare. STRAIGHT-TALKING and NANCY NO-FIERTY rush back on in alarm.

S-TALKING: Oh no!

NANCY: What's up?

S-TALKING: The Fourth Estate!
Straight-Talking – me! – they hate, can't wait
To dress me up in fancy frills
Or shoot me dead against a wall –

NANCY: Then you, dear friends, the Worthy Mob
Must bar the doors – come on, Braw Bob!

HUMANITY: And I, Humanity, must surely run for
If they come, Humanity's done for –

L&R: And Love and Respect must fly as well,
On me these Lords will cast a spell –

CHARITY: And as for charity, I'm off,
They sneer at Charity, they scoff
At every motive of the human heart,
Excepting greed –

EQUALITY: Aye, greed's their art:
For me, Equality, they don't give a fart!
And as for you, Democracy –

DEMOCRACY: Back to the North lands I must flee:
Religious bigots' domination
Of one poor fragment of this nation,
Intolerant rule by a slim majority,
Privilege enshrined, rich men's cupidity,
Ancient malpractice, lack of Constitution,
The evil of structural Destitution –
The Fourth Estaite approves quite happily
All in the name of me, Democracy –

26

If they come here to call the shots,
I'm off – they're just a pack of rats –

R-DEN: Good riddance, go, you moralising bores, –

CHARITY: We leave the stage to you, the whores.
You verbally-transmit disease
To help the power of the few increase
While old and poor folk bear the brunt
Of all the lies you choose to print!

G-G-J: Will ye no' come back? It grieves me sore
Tae see sic guid folk oot the door –

DEMOCRACY: We will come back, with gifts so many
If King Humanity weds your Jenny –

G-G-J: **(To HUM)** But you, good King, we need you so:
How can we ask you not to go?
I go on bended knees, I beg,
Don't leave us wi' these poisonous clegs!

HUMANITY: If here I stay I risk my life:
Corruption, scorn, Luxury, strife
The weapons they will use to kill,
And rule a foul, inhuman hell –

G-G-J: But here's a worthy mob, they're strong,
(To the audience) Ma' freens may fecht – or sing a song –
They know that Scotland won't be free
If from us Humanity's forced to flee –

HUMANITY: Very well – for you, I'll stay. Alone –
For these, my guardians, must be gone:
If I survive, they will return.

L & R: Humanity, you must run this risk;
For Scotland's sake, but all we ask,
Since your protection is our task,
You keep our cloaks around you set
In case you're tempted to forget.
If threatened in this land of thistle,
Just blow this piercing Freedom Whistle
And we'll rush back with love and solace
And ding your foes, like William Wallace!

HUMANITY: My thanks, farewell, Equality,
Love and Respect, Democracy,
And you my sweet Dame Charity:
I'll keep your whistle close to me.
I'll walk you north a little while
If we can't laugh, at least we'll smile . . .

MUSIC. They go, leaving their cloaks on four stands. As soon as they've gone, the FIVE MEDIAMEN conspire.

S-CARD: **(to S-DROOL)** Did you invite Lord Merde – och, he's –
    Our boss, our owner, one big cheese!

S-DROOL: Lord Merde? – Och aye – Pat, his PA:
    She said he's jetting here today
    To pick Jock's pockets, if he may . . .

S-SITCOM: **(sees cloaks)** Oh look, nice frocks, just lying round –
    I'll try one on **(Does, calls)** Look what I've found!

As the others discover the other cloaks, STRAIGHT-TALKING intervenes:

S-TALKING: I'm sorry, no, those can't be yours,
    They belong to good folk, no' to whores:

NANCY NO-FIERTY tries to take the cloak off SAL SITCOM:

NANCY: Aye, get it off, ye'll have it wreck'd
    That cloak's my mate's, Love and Respect!

R-DEN: Now not so fast, she's every right –
    Sal Sitcom shows us every night
    Respect and Love, what they are today:
    She's entitled to wear it, so I say! –
    For soaps and sitcoms teach our young
    To lead pure lives, tell right from wrong,
    So long as they cut out sex and swearing,
    Left-wing bias, artistic daring.
    Sal Sitcom, you can't be denied:
    Wear True Love's cloak, wear it with pride!

S-SITCOM: Sir Righteous Denunciation's right,
    I teach the young in sitcoms, soaps
    Every morning, afternoon and night
    Respect for glamour, to pin their hopes
    On make-up, hair-dos, wedding bands,
    The man they love must be bronzed, and golden,
    The girls all glossy, trendy blondes,
    Now chic and charm beguile your children.
    I teach them Love's new ABC,
    And Respect for due Authority!

SMART-CARD has found EQUALITY'S cloak – tries it on, turns, smiling:

S-CARD: I fancy this a little bit –
    It suits me, and it seems to fit –

Gives a twirl; NANCY goes for him.

NANCY: That cloak on you, don't make me puke!
    For that's Equality's coat you took!

S-CARD: Equality's the game I'm in!
    Equal rights to lose: or win!
    Equal rights – to buy up Sport for me,
    Then charge you for what once was free!
    To buy up movies, for a nice big slice,
    Then you can see them – at a price –
    And when you've bought your cheap little packet,
    And all the rights are in our pocket,
    You'll pay lots more! A lovely racket!
    On the old, elitist, BBC
    Such programmes did you ever see?

W. MOB: (**Yell**) Aye! Of course we did! Etc.

S-CARD: None of these benefits for you and me
    Can come without Equality –

He parades in the cloak – then RIGHTEOUS DENUNCIATION discovers DEMOCRACY's cloak, walks round it.

R-DEN: Well yes, I think Democracy's mantle
    Should fall on me, not on some disgruntled
    Anarchist or Trot appallin'
    Who aims to be a Tsar like Stalin –
    I'll try it on –

He struggles into DEMOCRACY's cloak, ripping it –

        A perfect fit,
    Perhaps a trifle tight, but yet
    I am the heir of Edmund Burke,
    Who blocked dread Danton's dreadful work
    And kept that Revolution there, in France,
    And made your Scottish gallows dance;
    Democracy's not the Rule of mobs –

WORTH MOB growls and protests –

    Only the Few can grasp it: not you slobs!
    It's special, cultured, calm, sedentary,
    Democracy is Parliamentary!
    And I, Sir Righteous Indignation
    Safeguard Westminster's best traditions –
    Secrecy, Deals, and Compromise,
    Misleading Half-Truth, never Lies,
    This culture up **my** flagpole climbs –
    You see, I write for the London Times,

Which is, in case you haven't heard
Owned by, and Organ of, Lord Merde!
I thunder wittily in my column
Against the Left; my prose turns solemn
As I blast the atheist, Nazi crooks
The Blairs, the Browns, the Robin Cooks:
They should be extinct, by Natural Selection,
Forbidden to stand in a democratic election!
(PONDERS) Perhaps that's too much, that drift to the Right:
Must take care not to give the dim voters a fright –
Let's just say they're not fit to govern our nation,
They lack civilised grace, they lack . . . moderation!
And that's how it works! That's democracy!
Like your NHS, it's quite safe with me!

STRAIGHT-TALKING stands glowering above and pointing at the statue of THATCHER.

S-TALKING: It's you's done this! Your weasel words
    Were laxative to a million turds:
    They poison-gas us, like Iraq the Kurds!

THATCHER'S VOICE, on tape, booms out:

THATCHER'S VOICE: 'Anything to do with the gassing of the Kurds . . .'

RIGHTEOUS DENUNCIATION rushes over, shoos STRAIGHT-TALKING away:

R-DEN: Now she knew nothing! Well, maybe she was told,
    But her memory's going, she's tired, she's old!
    Straight-Talking, like Tom, you're a frightful Paine,
    We don't want to hear your whinge again!

NANCY: Hey look! That bastard from the Sun,
    Just look at what he's trying on!

SLAVERING-DROOL has the cloak of CHARITY on, grinning broadly, strutting about.

S-DROOL: Tasty, no? Like the Sunday Sport!
    Now, come on, fair dos, noo, we support
    Your Charity Marathons, suchlike capers –
    A couple of quid can sell a million papers!
    And to denounce a miser mean
    We'll give a few inches down Page Sixteen –
    And **Labour** Meanness's a Front Page Story,
    We've even, once, attacked a Tory!
    See Divorcees whose Alimonies fail:
    We scream: Let's Throw Meanies into Jail!
    See me, see Charity – I'm all for it:

I'll show Lord Merde, och, he'll adore it:
To Tory Party Funds he gives
All the cash he can afford –
That's what crooks and rich old spivs
Must do to get to be a Lord!

S-TALKING: Slavering Drool, you're mean and nasty –
Get it off before I do something hasty –

S-DROOL: Nah. Charity – I think that's me
The soul of generosity!

S-TALKING: **(TO NANCY NO-FIERTY)** Our Nancy No-Fierty, we're in a fix
We've arrived at nineteen ninety-six:
Democracy, Equality, there's none,
Love and Respect with Charity have gone,
And in their places, hacks and phoneys
Who fill our minds with tripe, baloney:
Controlled by multi-national cash
How can Humanity survive this trash?

G-G-J: And will ma Jenny grow up right
Bombarded by this pile of shite?

NANCY: Will she be born, at all, or aborted
By their lies contorted and distorted,
Her amniotic fluid polluted,
The poor wean twisted in every direction
And now they tell her she's a misconception!

NOISES OFF.

S-TALKING: And here their masters come, the great,
The unelected Fourth Estaite –
Can we hope to survive this dreadful fate?

Scene 4

The Big Boys

More Oscar-type sumptuous fanfarollas, and the Entrance of the Lords of the Fourth Estate: SIR TERRESTRIAL MUNDANE, BART; and LORD TECHNO-CRASS, all making a great fuss, in big masks.

SIR TERRESTRIAL MUNDANE and LORD TECHNOCRASS crash around the audience bellowing:

SIR T-M: Is this the TV Festival? We're trying to find the George hotel! I say, – God they don't understand a blind word I'm saying, no wonder we can't show Scottish shows to our audience, they speak some totally incomprehensible language full of Goidelic grunts, and clicks like the Zulus – **(slowly)** Is this the way to the Television Festival?

LORD T: Can you direct us to the George Hotel? We're very important people, so you must make a really big effort!

SIR T-M: Are there no taxis in this town? I had to leave my driver in London, I'd better send for him to bring up the car!

LORD T: Is Gleneagles too far orf? At least you'll get a decent cup of tea at Gleneagles – Why can't we have the TV Conference at Gleneagles?

BRAWBOB: Bloody good idea!

SIR T-M has reached the forestage, calls to LORD T:

SIR T-M: This looks like us! Come up on the platform – You'll have to push through this smelly bunch of scum-bags – **(They growl at him)** Careful you don't catch AIDS, hold your nose and run!

LORD T makes it onto the stage, looks around. SIR T-M sees the audience, suddenly puts on full PR beam:

SIR T-M: I want you to know how delightful it is for you that we've come. Now – **(Takes out half-moons, reads from speech)**

    I am Sir Terrestrial Mundane, Burt, no Bart –
    Call me Terry, I'm just a young furt, no fart;
    Since television is the seventh art
        And much the best paid,
    An executive's got to be mobile, free
    To leave Channel 4 for the ITV,
    Then bid to be boss of the BBC –
        We got it made!
    To inform to teach to entertain
    That's our mission, but let's be plain
    Informing and teaching are a bit of a pain,
        For us, and you.
    If we make millions of punters switch on
    Who cares if the writers, producers bitch on,
    It's a reputation we can get rich on
        And status too.

LORD T bumbles up:

LORD T: Technocrass here, I hadn't planned
    To be any more than polite and bland –
    What I've got to say you won't understand,

So just nod your head . . .
We have the technology, believe what I say
To bring you fresh miracles every day –
The problem is this: you've got to pay,
    Or we're all dead.

We can bring you Video-on-Demand
Just phone BT with your command
And down your phone-line we can instantly send
    To your own TV:
And High Definition: you just can't wait
To buy a new telly, the picture's great!
We know you'll pay – or put it on the slate !
    You wait, you'll see.
Another channel you **know** you need,
So millions of videos won't work, take heed –
Then Channel 5 with repeats we'll feed
    To give you Choice:
And then there's the Digital Compress-i-on,
You'll get five hundred channels where once was one,
You'll buy it, the Market Research has been done – **(looks)**
    You've lost your voice . . .

STRAIGHT-TALKING emerges from his hiding-place:

S-TALKING: Are you the mighty Fourth Estaite?

SIR T-M: We are: we got here a little late
    And now we're thrown in a dreadful tizz –
    We're not quite sure which Festival this is!

S-TALKING: Well this is theatre –

SIR T-M: **(cynically)** I hear what you say . . .

NANCY: But unfortunately you are in the play!

LORD T: Us? In a piece of Guttenberg glitz?

SIR T-M: The very idea gives me the shits –

S-TALKING: We're none too keen, but your lackey insists!

SMART-CARD gets up, smiling hollowly, greets them:

S-CARD: Greetings Terry, Lord Technocrass,
    Now please ignore this Thespian ass:
    The fact is all the Powers in the Land
    Are gathered for some event they've planned,
    But forgot to invite both of you and Lord Merde,
    So we faxed in case you hadn't heard –
    If important people are gathered together

It's a great opportunity to lobby and blether:
And if I may be perhaps biting or mordant –
Lord Merde, even you, are far more important!

SIR T-M: But what's the event? And what's more, worst of all,
We're going to miss the TV Festival –
I'm down to lecture on Preparing for Labour
With a Question and Answer on Love Thy Neighbour.

LORD T: And I tell the assembled congregation
We must insist on DeRegulation –
No more constraints on what we can own
No pious control over what can be shown,

SIR T-M: We can't hang around with underpaid actors
We're the Nation's Conscience, the Lords Protectors –

S-CARD: I know, I know, but take your place!
Lord Merde approaches: His Amazing Grace!

A fanfarolla of Amazing Grace – an almost Papal figure, a Cardinal Richelieu of our times, appears, in full regalia, with a Rupert Murdoch mask on, preceded by altar-girls swinging incense-boats, others carrying candles, and a large crucifix on which is nailed the naked, smiling, pouting, figure of a Page Three girl, enters.

A Heavenly Choir sings Amazing Grace as this mini-Procession reaches the forestage. The crucifix is set up high on the set, facing the audience, and Lord MERDE proceeds to dominate the stage, planting himself firmly centre, holding his crook. He mutters to the altar-girls:

LORD M: Piss off, you're in me spotlight! **(They go. He calls to the WORTHY MOB)** Arseholes! Take this crook!

Two of the WORTHY MOB rush up and seize him.

Not me!
This holy crook, kindly lent by the RSC!

They take his crook off. He looks around.

That's beaut! **(Examines hall)** Nice place you folks have got:
I hear the Council's in a spot:
How's half a million for the whole job lot?
Hey Bruce! Where's Bruce?

(SMART-CARD appears)

Oh Bruce, you old blighter,
Relieve me of this weighty mitre:

(SMART-CARD takes off his mitre, removes it)

> Acquiring is my favourite sport –
> Divesting though of what you thought
> Might come in handy one fine day
> Is greater if some fool will pay
> More than you bought it for – Hey Bruce –
> Help get this poncey cape thing loose!

SMART-CARD takes off his huge cape, leaving him grey, balding, in vest and long Johns.

> That's better! now for a pint of Castlemaine! **(Gets one, drinks)**
> Lord Merde, he feels himself again! –
> But not in front of the children! HarHar!

A place has been set between SIR T-M and LORD T. They stand and immediately SIR T-M grabs his elbow and walks him around, speaking confidentially, with LORD T trying to hear.

SIR T-M: Lord Merde, old chap, how do you feel?
> Come sit by me, let's do a deal!
> Now if Her Majesty – God Save the Queen! –
> Should pop her clogs, it sets the scene
> For the television spectacular of our generation –
> Prince Charles! The Abbey! The Coronation!
> Now Merde, you old rogue, Rupert, Roop,
> We know you'd jump through every hoop
> To buy the rights for B Sky B,
> The Exclusive of the century!
> Now I hear the Palace want fifty million,
> With residuals rising to half a billion –
> And that's a price we can't afford;
> Consider, Rupert, noble Lord,
> If we withdraw our bid, what what!
> The price would have to drop a lot:
> Then you could snitch it, grab exclusive,
> Secure the prize that's so elusive,
> And for this favour, neat and sweet,
> You'd grant us a few clips and a cheap repeat!
> Our audience would cable up, buy dishes,
> You'd have all that your heart, your Newscorp wishes.
> And when our audience dwindles down to a few,
> I'll come and do the same for you:
> Chief Exec, a seat on the board:
> How does that grab you, of Merde the Lord?

LORD M: You ruthless, devious bastard, Gus:
> A shit like you should work for us!

SIR T-M: Oh thank you, Merde – but I'm not Gus –
> I'm Terry Mundane, soft but sussed . . .

LORD M: So who's this Gus?

SIR T-M: In Scottish Region
    There's such a man: his foes are legion,
    With claymore, dagger, broadsword, dirk
    They try to track this shabby burk,
    But off he vanishes, in mist and murk . . .
    Enough of him: my deal, Lord Merde?
    If that suits you, just say the word . . .

LORD M: I'll just consult me mates, the Board . . .

LORD T sidles up to LORD MERDE

LORD T: Now Merde, I'm Technocrass, a boffin –
    (confidential) Together we can nail him in his coffin:
    My wizardry, my ploys, my widgets,
    My deft compressing of the digits,
    My banks of Video-on-Demand,
    High Definition, that's all planned,
    Convergence, ah – the very word
    Leaves me trembling, shaken, stirred,
    Your phone, your video-store, your telly,
    Digitised, stored in your computer's belly;
    With CD-Roms and instant e-mail,
    Dial-a-Porn film, then Dial-a-Female,
    Next century's Multi-Media station
    In every home, in every nation!
    Are you still with me? Do I bore you?

LORD M: Keep talking, Prof, I'm there before you:
    If we invest, I think you mean,
    We'll scoop the market, up we'll clean!

LORD T: You've got it! It gives us incredible powers –
    We own the wrorld, it's ours, it's ours!

LORD M: Don't shout too loud, you're tempting fate:
    You'll make the bastards regulate!
    Just keep it bland, no Press, no noise –
    I'll run it by my back-room boys:

LORD T: I'm working on a prototype
    Avoiding any Media hype –

LORD M: World mind-control; if that's the prize
    Our profits rise and rise and rise!
    But enough your trying up to chat me –
    Who're all these pommies staring at me?
    What's going on? Why am I here?
    Did Bruce slip something in me beer?

If this is such a class event
Why was no invite ever sent?
So who's in charge? The government?

STRAIGHT-TALKING steps forward:

S-TALKING: Your lackeys thought you should drop by:
The Three Estaites were asked, but why
Imposters from the so-called Fourth Estaite
Should muscle in . . . Don't tempt me! Wait!
I'll bite my tongue, I'll hold my peace –

LORDM: What lackeys? I own none of these:
Own Love, own Charity, who me?
What prat is this – Equality?
Democracy? You're joking cobber,
They're all the things I'm trying to-clobber!

**SAL SITCOM, SLAVERING DROOL, SMART-CARD and RIGHTEOUS
DENUNCIATION dressed as LOVE & RESPECT, CHARITY, EQUALITY and
DEMOCRACY all stand up grinning –**

S-DROOL: We tricked you there: it's April Fool:
I'm no Charity, I'm Slavering Drool,
Your boy as fills the Scottish Sun
Wi' scandals, lies, wi' tit and bum!

S-SITCOM: And I'm Sal Sitcom, Lord, I buy
Your soaps, your sitcoms for your Sky:
Love and Respect's my little joke –
(Sidles up) By any chance would you fancy a furtive poke?

S-CARD: Smart-Card here, your Sky Exec:
I'd wring Equality's grubby neck,
But our disguises help us con
Her Majesty's loyal opposit-i-on,
Who soon may form the government –
It pays to keep them sweet, content.

R-DEN: Democracy leads to spiral Inflation:
But I'm Righteous Denunciation –
And when it seems we're about to lose,
Democracy we've learnt to use.
Democracy works: its magic powers
Keep Ulster British, Orange and ours,
And when the miners went on strike,
And didn't ballot – the strike we broke !
To castrate Unions, Democracy is the knife,
Democracy – in place of Strife !
The right to a brilliant lawyer's skill

If you've the cash means the right to kill,
The right to private medicine, schools,
The right to make up our own rules,
No Democrat would dare deny:
So I wear this cloak, and pigs can fly!

LORD M: You crafty bastards, right on, sports:
Your wheeze is brill: you've been well taught!
Keep up the work! **(aside)** Till, comes the dawn,
I'll throw you up – some rainbow yawn!

Claps hands.

But still I don't know what's going on?
Is this the Olympics? The Marathon?

G-G-JOCK: It's no'. It's a play. About Scotland's future:
A sortae allegorical adventure.
If ye want tae see it, sit ye doon:
Or go pollute some other toon.

LORD M: Scotland? I'll give you twenty minutes –
There may be a few pennies in it:

S-TALKING: Then take your places, hold your din:
The Play of Jenny's about to begin!

NANCY: No, no, we'll need to take a break,
Their bladders are bursting, their knee-joints ache:
I'll tell ye what: go down the bar,
Or take a walk, but don't go far,
Because I promise, in minutes just twenty
We'll begin the play as we was meant tae.
Yell see how Jenny's going to be born,
And grew up a maiden all forlorn
Until Humanity comes along
And fills her heart with love's sweet song -
There's something for everybody: That's the trailer,
Go grab a drink, or grab a sailor,
But come ye back here, laid or pissed -
For Scotland's story can't be missed!

But first! – let out the Four Estaites –
I beg you, for a moment wait –
These loons insist on pomp and state:
The worthy Mob will clear their route –
And then the rest of yous gets oot!
Music for a hollow parade –
A most pretentious serenade!

Glitz music as the WORTHY MOB go off up the aisle, again lacerating themselves with the cries as before: Scotland! Bannockbum! Etc.

They are followed by LORDS MERDE and TECHNOCRASS, SIR TERRESTRIAL MUNDANE, SIR RIGHTEOUS DENUNCIATION, SLAVERING DROOL, SAL SITCOM AND SMART-CARD.

STRAIGHT-TALKING, NANCY NO-FIERTY, AND GREAT GRANDAD JOCK go off into the wings after watching them go.

End of Act One

Act 2

During the Interval the foyer and bars have been serenaded from the speakers by the jingles from many ads. On the screens, more cable shopping channels, with interpolations: eg, a row of car commercials followed by shots of Kuwaiti oil-wells burning.

The audience are summoned back by the WORTHY MOB who go round beating drums to get them in, and yelling at them.

Scene 1

Re-entry of the Gladiators

Screen in the auditorium has been showing the ads etc, is now raised.

When the audience are in, the WORTHY MOB go round begging, hassling, performing bits of street-theatre, busking, etc.

STRAIGHT-TALKING comes striding in to start the show; with NANCY NO-FIERTY.

On the stage, the large figure of GRANDFATHER JOCK's daughter, NETTY MacPARTAN, who is a ten-foot high, very pregnant maquette.

S-TALKING: Welcome back, and now, I know,
    We promised you we'd start the show –
    So settle down, and take your ease,
    We'll do our best, we'll Aim To Please.

NANCY: Now this dame here is Netty McPartan –

BRAW BOBBY, near the front, interrupts, jumping up onto the steps at the front of the stage:

BRAW B: Come on, dig deep in your pockets, good folk,
    These people have no homes, and that's no joke
    In Embro's cold winter when the East wind blows,
    Pierces your bones, your frozen toes
    Drop off, your eyes gum up, your teeth
    Aye chitter, and from the Pentlands down to Leith
    You wander, seeking out a sheltered nook,
    And yet you're treated like some scabby crook
    When none of us are homeless by oor ain choice –
    If you lose your home, you lose your voice:

There's some are sick, some unemployed
Some slash their wrists, can't face the void:
Aye, some take drugs, a desperate measure
To buy a buzz, to die for pleasure –
But we are a' Jock Tamson's bairns,
Tho' we must lose while your speculator earns
Enough for fifty with his taxes cut
Tae 'decrease the burden on the State' –
That's us, by the way! Burden! Great!

STRAIGHT TALKING interrupts:

S-TALKING: Very good, Braw Bob, you've had your say,
    Now please can we begin the play?

BRAW B: I've had this Paradise, this Tory Eden –
    Lend's the fare for a ferry to Stockholm, Sweden?
    Or Norway, Denmark, somewhere Scandic –
    I'd even try to learn Icelandic:
    Their poor don't live on the streets in fear,
    And yet they're doing far better than we are –

S-TALKING: So help me Bob, ye're off again
    Ye're girnin' like a dripping drain!
    Ye're right, correct, now hold your stricture
    Till we have shown the wider picture!

BRAW B: The wider picture! Why and how?
    They need a house, and they need it now:
    OK – I've done – let's see the show. . .

As BRAW BOBBY and the WORTHY MOB take their places, SLAVERING DROOL dressed as Charity, SIR RIGHTEOUS DUNUNCIATION as Democracy, BRUCE SMART-CARD as Equality and SAL SITCOM as Love and Respect come bustling in wiping their mouths with napkins, burping, a bit tipsy, burbling on about the excellent dinner and wines they've had.

SMART-CARD waves at STRAIGHT-TALKING:

S-CARD: They're on their way, they've had their fill,
    Lord Merde, our host, is settling the bill –

Noises off.

    Ah here they come, arrange some chairs,
    Along the front, say there, and there!

The Stage Manager comes on with three folding canvas chairs, and is a little worried to be putting them up right across the audience.

The WORTHY MOB protest. The Stage Manager hesitates –

S-CARD: Terrific, Fine!

BRAW B: You've blocked our view!
    And these folk have paid: Some sponsors too!

S-CARD: Sponsors! For this! I beg to stay cynical –
    Who'd sponsor a show whose psychosis is clinical!
    And as for the punters, they're quite content
    For us to come between them and this event,
    You see, they need us to interpret reality
    They don't have the time, let alone the ability –
    We are the media, their ears, their eyes,
    We mediate truth into acceptable lies
    We set the agenda, carefully choose
    What needs to be known, the suitable news.
    So they don't need to **see** it, blow by blow,
    We'll edit and give them what's fit to show!

NANCY NO-FIERTY herself sweeps up the chairs and dumps them at the side.

NANCY: The game's a bogey, ye're out of order!
    That may work in England – no' North o' the Border!
    Ye'll no inflict your subservient habit –
    In Scotland we say: Let the Dog see the Rabbit!

S-TALKING: Blow the trumpets, Bring them in,
    For any's sake let this show begin!

Scene 2

The Play actually begins

More Amazing Grace, soupy, and Enter LORD MERDE, still in vest and long-johns, SIR TERRESTRIAL-MUNDANE, and LORD TECHNOCRATS.

LORD MERDE goes stage-centre where his seat was, and plonks himself down without looking. There is no seat. He bellows.

LORD M: Bruce! Where's me seat? I've come to this farce
    And everybody knows what the next rhyme's gonna be
    So I won't say it, – Give me a hand up, Smart-Card!

S-CARD: This forward young woman, Your Amazing Graces,
    Has decided to put us all in our places,
    Over here, at the side, please forgive the indignity
    But the Scots are over-flowing with spite and malignity!

LORD M: That'll do, come on Technocrass, Terry, let's sit
And prepare to receive this whole crock of – wit!

They sit.

STRAIGHT-TALKING and NANCY NO-FIERTY come to announcing positions tentatively, can't believe they're not being interrupted, and begin:

NANCY: Can we begin?

S-TALKING: Well no-one's stopped us –

NANCY: It's worse than coitus interruptus!

S-TALKING: Let's go, let's go, the coast is clear

NANCY: If we don't go now, we'll be here next year!

STRAIGHT-TALKING steps forward, begins:

S-TALKING: So settle down and take your ease,
We'll do our best, we Aim To Please –

NANCY: Now this dame here is Netty MacPartan,
A Stoic heroic, a Tartan Spartan –
Since 1707 she's been with child,
And in her womb the child goes wild –
She's mad to be out, her ma's keen too,
For Netty is carrying Scotland the New!

LORD MERDE gets up, examines Netty, turns to his cohorts who are seated around.

LORD M: Did you hear that? A new-born Scotland:
I'm livin' in Somebody-ought-to-be-Shot-land –
Why didn't you bastards send me a wire –
We must support them so our sales go higher!

S-DROOL: Dinnae fash yersel', my noble Lord –
The Scottish Sun's readership's already soared,
We said Vote Nat, Be Proud ye're a Scot,
Set Scotland Free: we sold a lot. . .

LORD M: I'm pleased to hear it, Slavering Drool,
I'm glad to see you're nobody's fool:
If that's the band-wagon, jump on –

R-DENUN: But is it, when all's said and done,
In our best interests: Scotland votes Labour –

LORD M: And Labour rules by my grace and favour!
Wise up, Sir Righteous Denunciation,
It's *we* who decide what goes in this nation!
If Scotland's too red, we'll question her sanity –

S-CARD: But she'll probably wed this 'King Humanity!'
   If he's her consort, his ghastly friends
   Whose cloaks we wear his ear will bend, –

R-DENUN: My point exactly! Next thing you'll see
   The Scots demanding Equality,
   Love and Respect, Charity,
   And worst of all – Democracy!

LORD M: Ye're right! Those moralising hypocrites!
   They make me chunder, give me the shits!

S-SITCOM: But, Lord and Master, Twentieth-century fox,
   'Tis **we** who wear their magic cloaks!
   If **we** advise Humanity fair
   And warn him he must have a care –
   That if he marries this pert lass,
   Calamity will come to pass!

LORD M: Good thinking, Sitcom, take a raise –

S-SITCOM: How can I thank you for such praise?

S-DROOL: I've got it! I hear wedding bells!
   We'll get him to marry someone else!

R-DENUN: But who?

S-CARD: Yes, who?

S-DROOL: I'll be back in a tick –
   Gloria Cupsize: she'll do the trick!
   You've had it, King Humanity –
   No man resists a Great Page Three!

S-SITCOM: I hear him coming –

S-DROOL: I'm forae aff!
   When I get back, wes'll have a laugh!

He slips off, as a fanfare (and another StepDance?) announces the arrival of HUMANITY, somewhat forlorn.

The FOURTH ESTATE, – MERDE, TECHNOCRASS and SIR T MUNDANE back off and sit down at the side.

RIGHTEOUS DENUNCIATION, SMART-CARD and SAL SITCOM, in their cloaks, sit on the chairs previously occupied by Democracy, Equality and Respect & Love, quite still, like statues.

HUMANITY sees only their cloaks and the back of their heads, and is amazed, goes to greet them warmly:

HUMANITY: My friends! How come you're back so soon?

I thought I left you travelling north from Scone?
I'm overjoyed to see you back, but what way
Did you overtake me? I stopped by the Tay.
To honour McGonagle's silvery ghost,
And to buy my copy of The Sunday Post,
You must have passed me then: but why
Come back and run the risk you'll die?
And where is Charity, oh has she fled,
Or gone up North – or is she dead?

R-DENUN, SAL SITCOM and SMART-CARD all try to sound like the characters they are impersonating, but aren't very convincing.

R-DENUN: **(like Democracy)** Oh no, not dead, but gone to find
A partner to bring you peace of mind,
A maiden fair, comely and sweet,
With the biggest, er, heart, you'd hope to meet –

HUMANITY: But Charity knows fine I'm sworn
To stay quite free till Scotland's born –

R-DENUN: Come on, come on, that's hardly is it
The truly democratic spirit?

S-CARD: **(as Equality)** And as Equality I'm bound to note
Pre-judging does not get my vote –

S-SITCOM: **(as Love & Respect)** True Love demands an open heart,
Respect for all, for Saint, for Tart,
Humanity, please close no doors –
This girl could be for ever yours . . .

HUMANITY is confused, and not too sure about what's going on.

HUMANITY: My friends, your words I'm sure are wise –

S-DROOL: **(as Charity)** rushes in, doesn't take in HUMANITY, blurts out, excited:

S-DROOL: She's on her way, Ms G Cupsize!

They indicate HUMANITY. He goes into a pose as Charity.

My Lord, King Hum, you soon will see,
Brought to you out of Charity,
The perfect woman, pure Page Three!
She's Ersatz Sexuality –

Scene 3

Gloria struts her stuff

MUSIC. Smoke. Lights. As the smoke disperses, we see, high up, in bikini and stilettos, the curvaceous figure of GLORIA CUPSIZE, smiling, posing in a series of pert poses as for the camera.

HUMANITY can't help rising to the occasion as she moves provocatively closer. Her routine and the music pause, hold –

HUMANITY: I'm not so stupid, I know your game –
    But I can't resist you: what is your name . . . ?

MUSIC behind all this.

G CUPSIZE: I'm the juicy bait
    of the Fourth Estaite,
    The sweet Queen Bee
    Of your Page Three:
    I'm Gloria Cupsize
    So all you guys
    Come feast your eyes
    On breasts and thighs –
    And Fantasize:
    Deep breathing, sighs
    And little cries . . .
    Just watch it rise –
    For the circulation
    Is my consummation.

Dances

    I'm coy, I'm pert
    I'll lift my skirt
    I'll pout my lips
    I'll pose with whips
    I'll squeeze a breast
    Men like that best,
    My butt I'll bare
    To spank or tear:
    Feel free to rape her,
    She's only paper.

She dances.

    The real me
    Costs more to see
    But live striptease

Could never please
So many men
As in The Sun,
The Star, The Mirror,
With Shock and Horror!
When a camera clicks
On my sly tricks
I swell with pride
I've satisfied
With pelvic thrust
And bouncing bust
A nation's lust.

MUSIC changes to softer, more sentimental. She seduces HUMANITY.

But what I long for
Come on strong for, –
I yearn to try
To love one guy,
To him I'd bring
My everything:

She langorously demonstrates to HUMANITY:

My breasts, my thighs
Just for his eyes,
My body trim
Just for him,
My lips I'd pout
My butt stick out,
My wicked glance
Provocative stance,
My squeals, my groans
For him alone.

She wraps herself round HUMANITY.

Yes, if you wish
My dainty dish
Is yours to chew . . .
That man . . . Is You . . .

HUMANITY: **(to audience)** Humanity is only human:
I can't say No to such a woman.
But Jenny, Scotland, Grandpa Jock –
(to G-CUPSIZE) I need to pause, to think, take stock . . .

G-CUPSIZE: Don't hesitate,
Don't make me wait –
Come play with me

> Your own Page Three
> Let's go, explore,
> There's so much more
> Than in, it seems,
> Your wildest dreams . . .
> But take me soon
> Or I'll be gone
> Ten million men
> Would kill to win
> Their dream, the prize:
> Me, Gloria Cupsize!

HUMANITY: I ponder, pause, not to insult,
> But if these friends I may consult
> Then I'll more surely plight my troth
> And with glad heart I'll take the oath –
> You'll dedicate yourself to me
> And I to you with certainty . . .

GLORIA CUPSIZE looks at the Four Imposters, who smile and nod to her.

G-CUPSIZE: My Lord, I obey:
> Whatever you say –

HUMANITY: But stay quite near

G-CUPSIZE: I shall, never fear. . . .
> I'm longing, yearning
> My flesh is burning –
> I just can't wait . . .

HUMANITY: Then, contemplate!

He goes over to S-DROOL, who is dressed as Charity.

HUMANITY: Dame Charity, have sympathy
> On love-torn lovers such as me
> Pulled between lust and fidelity
> > To vows I've sworn –
> There's not one man, nor woman here
> Who's never felt this tug, this war,
> Lies down in heaven, but wakes to fear
> > The light of dawn. . . .

S-DROOL: Oh no, oh no, that's Calvin's guilt,
> To love the way a woman's built
> Is not a crime: your joys all wilt
> > If you say no:
> Your fleshly pleasures you must take
> When up for grabs: just eat your cake,

Munch every crumb. Do not forsake
    Your libido . . .

For pleasuring these days must be
Acquired for cash, a commodity,
Now nothing can be had for free –
    It's no disgrace:
The spirit of the age is this:
Each touch, each stroke, carress and kiss
Are traded in that bower of bliss,
    The market place. . . .

HUMANITY: But Jenny and Scotland and Grandpa Jock?

S-DROOL: A man can't put his life in hock,
    Deny his heart, in case he'll break
        Some ancient habits:
    Get stuck in, son, she's sonsy, stacked,
    You can't have all your chances wrecked
    To end up trapped. Come on, defect,
        Go to, like rabbits!

HUMANITY nods, confused, goes to SIR RIGHTEOUS DENUNCIATION, dressed as Democracy.

HUMANITY: This Charity is strange but true –
    Democracy, now what say you?

R-DENUN: Something borrowed, something blue
        Is my advice:
    To spurn a frame so lean, athletic
    Could not be known as democratic,
    Nor enterprising, plain pathetic,
        Not very nice. . . .

HUMANITY turns questioning to SMART-CARD dressed as Equality.

HUMANITY: Equality?

S-CARD: You're such a snob,
    Stop acting like some priggish slob
    Get off the pot and on the job
        You weak-kneed pisser –
    This Welfare State's destroyed your drives –
    What's wrong with going at it like knives?
    You're not a pussy with nine lives,
        Go on and kiss her –

HUMANITY turns to SAL SITCOM, as Love & Respect.

HUMANITY: My trusted friend, Love and Respect,
    Should I some different words expect

From you whom all who love elect
    Queen of their hearts?
I feel within a queasy feeling,
My heart is sore, my senses reeling,
A shadow falls, a fear comes stealing,
    My conscience smarts –

S-SITCOM: Oh sweet young person, charming boy,
    These fears are sent to try, annoy
    The lover in pursuit of joy
        And lasting pleasure:
    Your feelings and your conscience clear
    Do credit to you. Have no fear.
    These scruples will soon disappear:
        You'll have your treasure –

    If true love smoothly ran its course
    There'd be no drama, no divorce,
    Our lives without some spice, some sauce,
        Would bore us rigid:
    For love means turmoil, passion, pain
    See Mimi's Paris, Carmen's Spain –
    East Enders' London, Neighbours' terrain;
        For calm read frigid . . .

HUMANITY is in a turmoil, paces around. As he approaches GLORIA she smiles and preens. He turns away.

HUMANITY: What should I do? Make Gloria mine?
    Or wait for Jenny to be born?
    If Gloria's delights I grasp
    Will she, like Cleopatra's asp
    Cling to my breast, then pierce and poison?
    Dead, before I even clap eyes on
    This wondrous land, this new beginning?
    How shall I know? My head is spinning . . .
    And yet these friends I love and trust
    Say: Go For Gloria, obey your lust
    Remember man returns to dust
    And fall on Cupsize ample bust . . .
    I'm lost, I must, I can't resist . . .

As he goes towards a welcoming GLORIA, enter, driving him back, the TWELVE STEP-DANCERS, with rhythmic attack. They do a few routines then stop.

One of them, ANNIE, steps towards him:

ANNIE: If that treacherous slapper you should wed
    You're round the bend, you're off your head:

Scotland's future needs Humanity
To keep us fit, preserve our sanity:
We are that future, and we say:
Just be there, son: alright? OK?

They step-dance off. He follows them off, but GRANDPA JOCK arrives behind him, alone, and laughs:

G-JOCK: You like the lassies? But haud on, steady –
Ye're promised to my lovely Jenny!

HUMANITY: Great-grandpa Jock, all I can see
Is Sensuous Gloria from Page Three,
A male erotic fantasy
And she, she says, is all for me!

GRANDPA JOCK goes and inspects her, incredulous.

G-JOCK: Oh jings, oh crivens, stretch my condom –

He looks around suspiciously –

But this encounter's far frae random:
This mound of flesh is surely sent
Tae lure ye frae yer chief intent,
A decoy, duck, a Mata Hari, –

GJ goes to GLORIA CUPSIZE

Who sent ye here? D'you plan to marry
A man like him – Humanity? Harry?

G CUPSIZE: Well, yes, I think –
He's such a hunk –
He's mine, all lovely,
He tastes like bubbly
Pink champagne:
I can't complain,
He's not a slob.
A job's a job . . .

GJ: A job? Whose pay-roll pays your bill?
What sugar-daddy fills your till?

G CUPSIZE: Did I say that?
No, I did not!

She turns to HUMANITY, very seductively:

My gorgeous man
Come fill my can

A Satire of the Four Estates

I'm open wide:
Did you decide?

HUMANITY: I can't say No –

GGJ: You cannae say Yes!

HUMANITY: I will! – Perhaps –

GGJ: Oh what a mess!
What lies below her painted beauty?
Remember Jenny, do your duty!

HUMANITY: You're right. I can't. There's more to life

LORD MERDE, angry, gets up, pushes GGJ aside:

MERDE: You'll take this Sheila for your wife!
She's beaut, she's curvy, sexy, – cor!
And with her comes a whole lot more!
You marry Gloria, you'll go far,
Some kids, a mortgage, family car,
Two weeks in Turkey, right-wing views,
A bit on the side: what you got to lose?

(sings) No ambition,
Got no Life
You got no choice
So you got no strife –
You got the Sun in the morning
and the Sky at night,
You got the Sun in the morning
and Sky in the evening
So you're alright . . .

LORD MERDE beckons GLORIA CUPSIZE forward. She comes, sultry. GREAT-GRANDPA JOCK tries to intervene, but LORD MERDE stops him.

Stay out of this, Granpa, –

GGJ: I'll no cower –

MERDE: We've got the money, we've got the power . . .

GREAT GRANDPA JOCK retreats as LORD MERDE drives him away:

Gloria Cupsize will you take this guy
To have, to hold, to own, to buy?

G CUPSIZE: I will . . .

MERDE: And do you, take this luscious bloom
To pay her bills, her life consume?

HUMANITY: I think so. But it might be fun
    If we could have a trial run:
    I fancy her, I think she's great,
    But something makes me hesitate,
    So if it's all the same to you
    It's Malta for a week, for two –

GREAT-GRANDPA JOCK is in despair. He turns to the 3 ESTAITES:

GGJ: Oh no! We're lost, poor Scotland the New
    Humanity never has proved true!
    In Russia's great experiment
    Humanity turned false and went,
    In China for Humanity's cause
    They fought, but soon he fled, and worse,
    America the Brave, embraced him,
    But after fifty years they lost him:
    Humanity, be constant, stay,
    We need you here, right here, today . . .

MERDE: Just shut your face, please cut the blether,
    The happy pair now leave, together –

He drives GREAT-GRANDPA JOCK off.

The 4 IMPOSTERS rise to wave them off, and dress them for the holiday!

R-DENUNCIATION gives huge Duty-Free bags –

R-DENUN: God speed them, says Democracy,
    Consume, consume, and you'll be free!

SLAVERING DROOL gives an Ann Summers catalogue.

S-DROOL: Love says: Enjoy! to the happy couple,
    Keep limbs, emotions, morals, supple!

SMART-CARD gives them portable TV sets –

S-CARD: You can receive us in Select Hotels –
    Keep viewing! Soon: It's wedding bells!

SAL SITCOM gives them their tickets, S-DROOL takes photo of them holding them.

S-SITCOM: Good luck, enjoy our Gloria's favours,
    Respect authority: Love Thy Neighbours –

HUMANITY and GLORIA CUPSIZE go off to Malta for a week's package holiday. LORD MERDE congratulates the IMPOSTERS, as they move off to the side.

Scene 4

Jenny is born

GREAT-GRANDPA JOCK comes back on, looks around. Questions STRAIGHT-TALKING and NANCY NO-FIERTY.

GGJ: They've done it?

NANCY: Aye! Not to the altar,
    Just a week's free trial, in Malta.

GGJ: What will we do? Braw Bobbie, son,
    Did you allow this tae be done?

B-BOBBIE: We did, we're scunnered wi' Humanity,
    We let him go – he's no use tae me . . .

GGJ: Wi'oot him ye're a bunch of thieves –
    What future when Humanity leaves?

S-TALKING: He's coming back – perhaps he'll find
    Gloria's consumables best left behind?

GGJ: He hasnae chosen?

S-TALKING: No, not quite –

GGJ: Then maybe it's no' quite too late – **(Ponders)**
    I have it! A surprise on his return –
    If he could see our Jenny, born,
    He'd fall in love, with fever'd brow
    Forget that other –

S-TALKING: Aye, but how?
    For part of Scotland's nemesis is
    She can't do parthenogenesis –

NANCY: That's a big word, a mighty yelp –

S-TALKING: It's means poor Nettie needs some help.
    There's midwives knocking at the door
    For near enough two hundred year,
    But none have quite induced the wean,
    Though forceps have been tried in vain,
    And Netty's too weak to take a Caesar:
    There's only one way to release her –

NANCY: What's that?

S-TALKING: A mighty thunderous shout
    And Jenny will come thundering out!

G-G JOCK: She'll no come oot, we'oot a shoot?
  (To audience) Ma freens, nae doot, ye'll help us oot!

From inside NETTY, JENNY can be heard singing 'Scots Wha Hae'.

G-G JOCK: (over) Oh, d'ye hear, she's singing, puir wee soul,
  She needs tae breathe, she canna' thole
  The dim dark womb, the prison-door shut,
  The umbilical chord, she needs it cut!

JENNY is still singing. He listens.

  D'ye hear? Her voice sae clean, and pure –
  It's more than mortal can endure –
  (To WORTHY MOB, and to audience)
  She's locked inside a living hell:
  So will ye shout? Just one big yell?

WORTHY MOB say 'Aye', 'We will', 'We'll give it a go' etc.
  (To audience) And you ma freens, one word, ye see,
  Can set ma Jenny, and Scotland, free –
  Even you English Tories, ye'll be in the ascendant,
  Wi' Scotland free, you'll be Independent!
  What will we shout, noo let me ponder . . .

JENNY is still singing –

  What word tae choose to roar like thunder?
  ⌐Freedom? Too corny, Hollywood's done it –
  Out? No, it's over before ye've begun it –
  Scotland? No. Thrust? No, a wee bit too phallic –
  I have it! Shout "Alba!" – that's Scotland in Gaelic!!
  Let's gie it a shottie, – it's Al-a-ba, right,
  Shout Al-a-ba, Al-a-ba, wi' all of your might!

Noo, ye'll need a rehearsal. Let me see – if I say 1-2-3, then ye'll shout
  altogether, will ye? Let's gie it a shottie: After 3 – 1-2-3: (Some shout) Again:
  1-2-3: (shouts). Hopeless – what am I daein' wrang?

BRAW B: Ye're pre-historic! Ye must dae the Count Canaveral! (Turns to
  audience) Is that no right? A' thegither! 10-9-8-7-6-5-4-3-2-1- ALABA!!

G-G JOCK: Magic! Noo if we dae that again and ye push up the umbrella as well,
  – like this (he shows) – Netty here will be so scared she'll have a baby! So
  let's see if we can't put her at least in Labour! So :
  10-9-8-7-6-5-4-3-2-1 – ALABA!!

**NETTY'S skirts begin to rise. An umbrella mechanism operates, opening and
swelling –she roars with a Labour pain – And the singing soars higher and
louder**

G-G JOCK: This time! This time! All at the pitch of your voices, and up with the
    umbrella!
    10-9-8-7-6-5-4-3-2-1- ALABA!!!

**And the umbrella goes up, and JENNY MacREDDIE steps out, surrounded by
the DANCERS who step dance aside to reveal her: she is 22, a Tartan
nightmare. At the end, applause, cheers from the WORTHY MOB. During
this, Netty the Umbrella vanishes, and JENNY takes her bow.**

G-G JOCK: Jenny MacReddie, my darling grand daughter
    As sweet and pure as pure spring water,
    My bonnie wee doo, ma douce wee doe,
    Ma woodie, ma hoodie, ma leaping roe,
    You've come into the world's harsh light,
    At last, at last, what a wonderful sight!
    Out of the womb of Netty MacPartan —
    But why are you wearing this bum-bee Tartan?

JENNY: Grandfather Jock, to be borne is pure heaven,
    When you've been in the womb since 17-oh-7,
    To see the world, these wonderful guys,
    The sight of such babes brings tears to my eyes,
    Such beautiful women, boys and girls,
    Come to see, like me, how my fate unfurls —
    Oh Brave New World, — but could it turn ugly?
    Is it Shakespeare's dream or the nightmare of Huxley?
    This tartan, you ask, is not my mother's
    But a plaid from each of my seven proud fathers:

    The first was a Pict, Bruide the King
    The Matriarch's son, who tried to bring
    From Forth to Orkney under his wing,
        Unite the east;
    My second the giant Finn McCuill
    Whose Mighty Deeds you learn at school,
    From Wicklow to Lewis Finn once ruled,
        Both King and priest.

    The third of my fathers was rough, unruly,
    But still rules many: the Orangeman, Billy,
    Whose head was aflame, whose heart is still chilly,
        With No Surrender;
    My fourth old dad tells tales, sings songs,
    Like Don Quixote goes righting wrongs
    But Charlie's pleasure did not last long:
        The Great Pretender

    My fifth the rebel-poet Burns
    The plough-boy whose sweet verses yearn
    For Liberty, Love, and for him earn

The nation's heart;
Kier Hardie next, the collier-lad,
Home-Rule he fought for, that old dad,
For Votes for Women he gave all he had,
    He played his part.

My last is John Maclean who died
Rather than swallow Scotland's pride,
Hero, teacher, who reddened the Clyde,
    No compromiser:
All these my fathers, and some others,
Some brave, some bullies, some stupid, some lovers,
But the love I need, is hers, my mother's:
    None wiser.

She turns to the DANCERS

Now you, my friends, I must command
To search all corners of this land
And find wise counsellors to advise
On how best Scotland may arise,
What principles should guide our future,
Draw out the best in human nature,
Arrange our polity so Scotland thrives
And **all** lead happy, fruitful lives –

**The DANCERS do a brief step of agreement and rush off in all directions.
GREAT GRANDPA JOCK examines her tartans.**

G-G JOCK: Your bumbee plaids are aye symbolic
    But remind me of Scotland the alcoholic,
    The year two thousand's chapping the door –
    We cannae live in the past any more:
    So come wi' me, down Princes Street,
    Tae French Connection, it'll be my treat,
    Tae get some gear, some nifty knix
    Tae wear in 1996!

JENNY: You're on, you're great, that's ace, that's barry

G-G JOCK: And then we'll see aboot who ye'll marry –

JENNY: What! Dress me like Best End of Lamb
    To sell along wi' haggis and ham!
    I intend to stay just like I am!

G-G JOCK: It's no' tae put ye up for sale –

JENNY: I'll no' dress up for some daft male!

G-G JOCK: Ye'll need to be more up-to-date:
    Just look at me, my sorry state –

I'm auld, decrepit, shelf-life over,
I canne thrive in an uncertain future,
But you, ma darlin', you must learn to cope:
If we're tae survive, ye're our only hope –
And looking backward's no the way
Tae flourish in the world the day!

JENNY: OK, OK, OK, OK:
The French Connection, did you say?

G-G JOCK: I did. Come on! My bonnie girl:
Try on a frock, and give us a twirl!

G-G JOCK and JENNY go off.

Scene 5

The plot sickens

BRAW BOBBIE goes onstage, sees nothing's happening:

B BOBBIE: If yous don't mind, I'd like to take this opportunity to introduce myself and my pals here, we've been very patient watching the capers goin' on up here, but, well, you cannae ignore us all bloody night, so please could we have a big hand for the boys and girls – you'd better try harder, a bigger hand, if you don't you'll have to buy The Big Issue every day for a year and a half, because you are the bourgeoisie and we, by the way, are The Underclasses – so let's hear it! Thank you, Thank you. We speak prose, by the way, no' verse – we're Low Life, so we don't rhyme. Now, here's they people: the great unwashed, the diseased, the derelicts, the alchies and the misfits – let me introduce them –

(THIS SPEECH TO BE RESEARCHED. IT ENDS, THEN:) Oh Christ, I'd best wrap up, time to sink back to the Lower Depths – I can hear Lover-Boy and his slag back from their test-drive – I'll let you get on – See you later!

A downbeat fanfare, and enter GLORIA, now with short, mannish hair, power shoulders, a great suit and a very business-like stride.

G CUPSIZE: (Calls, imperious) Merde! Lord Merde! You Fourth Estaite!

They appear, LORD MERDE, LORD TECHNOCRASS and SIR TERRESTRIAL-MUNDANE – surprised.

We need to talk – negotiate!

MERDE: It's Gloria, back –

SIR T-M: Are you to be wed?

LORD T: Technically satisfactory?

MERDE: Great in bed?

G CUPSIZE: I've done the job – no joy, no sorrow:
    If! say yes, we'll wed tomorrow –

MERDE: Bramah Gloria, – what a Sheila!

G CUPSIZE: Not so fast, Lord Wheeler-Dealer:
    Your Slavering-Drool-man promised me,
    A truly multinational fee –
    I don't want marriage, not for free!

MERDE: **(Taking her off)** Let's step outside, let's get some air,
    I'm sure we'll find a price that's fair –
    You're looking good – I like the hair –

He winks to SIR TERRESTRIAL-MUNDANE AND LORD TECHNOCRASS, who follow them off.

Enter an exhausted HUMANITY with silly sunglasses and straw hat, laden with extra luggage. He is tired and depressed. He sings:

HUMANITY'S song:

    My key won't turn anymore in the lock,
    And time moves backwards on my clock,
    My shoes don't fit, they're on the wrong feet,
    My heart won't beat, I'm incomplete
        In the Safeways of love . . .

    The shelves are stacked, the goods piled high,
    My trolley's full but I don't know why
    My appetite has gone away.
    My stomach churns, my cheeks are grey
        In the Safeways of love . . .

    For the time has passed
    For a love that lasts
    Like a pen of plast-
        ic it's disposable:
    When packaging
    Means everything,
    Love's a throwaway hang-
        kie it's unusable –

    The sun has set
    On Juliet –
    She'll soon forget
        Her Romeo
    She's not afraid:

> She'll choose a fad-
> -ed copy made
>   By Roneo . . .

JENNY comes in, in her new gear, looking very 1996 and stunning. The music gets pleased as HUMANITY sees her and thinks she's unbelievably wonderful. After they catch each other's eye, she turns away, also quite struck, as he sings:

> What happened to my heart, was that a beat?
> I see my future walking down the street –
> It's check-out time, the tills ring out
>   In the supermarket of love . . .
> No more cut-price beef, those days are done,
> No more special offers, life's begun,
> No more swirling head, no heart of stone –
> No packaged sprouts, I'll grow my own . . .
>
> **(speaks more normally)** Hello. Who are you?

JENNY: Jenny – and you?

HUMANITY: I'm Humanity – King once – now
    In exile, no home, no throne, just plain Harry . . .

JENNY: I see. When you were king – did you ever marry?

HUMANITY: Well no –

JENNY: **(moving closer)** That's great, that's brill, that's barry!
    See me, I'm Scotland, newly born
    I'm all alone, I'm all forlorn,
    I need a mate to share my life:
    Did you ever think you'd like a wife?

HUMANITY: I did, but – **(He stops, dejected)**

JENNY can see he's depressed. She takes him gently by the hand –

JENNY: Wait! Let me just show
    From up this hill the land below:

MUSIC, as they climb high.

> From Sullom Voe to Solway Firth
> This land is glistening at its birth,
> The lochs are leaping, Munroes tremble
> As Scotland's clans arise, assemble,
> The Gaeltacht sings, the Western Isles,
> See Highland faces wreathed in smiles,
> While old Dalriada stretches a hand,
> And Galloway dances along the strand,

Cairngorm and Grampian, Don and Speyside
Leave their sorrows along the wayside
And Tay and Forth their shores carress
While Nessie reels round Inverness,
And Glasgow rocks in Glasgow's fashion,
So cool and yet aflame with passion,
The Lothian acres primp and preen
With tender shoots of spring so green,
And Embra's bells and guns ring out
From close and vennel comes a shout:
Scotland is Born, to take her place
Among the orders of the human race,
To see her now, so young, so free,
So full of hope, such dignity,
The thrill of what she'll be and do −
I love her − so, my friend, do you?

HUMANITY: Who could resist, who dare say no:
This sight has set my heart aglow,
And you, sweet Jenny, this land's spirit
Are more than I could hope to merit −
But, well-advised by trusted friends, −
I'm promised: there the story ends.

JENNY: Promised? Engaged?

HUMANITY: Gloria's her name −
A Page-Three beauty, a sexy dame,
Although, perhaps, she's playing some game,
We've tried each other, she's changed me
Into this strange creature you see:
But what can I do? I gave my word,
But now I know that's quite absurd . . .

JENNY: A Page-Three beauty? You're to wed?

HUMANITY: I think so. Anyway: that's what I said . . .

JENNY: Without Humanity, Scotland's dead!

They move a long way apart.

HUMANITY: But −

JENNY: But?

HUMANITY holds out a hand. They move closer together as they say more and more fervently: 'But − '
Finally their fingers touch, and electricity crackles − Then:

61

Scene 6

Lord Merde and his Boys v Jenny

A huge Oscar-ish fanfare: Re-enter the FOURTH ESTAITE, LORDS MERDE and TECHNOCRASS, SIR TERRESTRIAL-MUNDANE, SLAVERING-DROOL as Charity, SMART-CARD as Equality, SIR RIGHTEOUS DENUNCIATION as Democracy and SAL SITCOM as Love & Respect.

On the hills STRAIGHT-TALKING and NANCY NO-FIERTY appear.

JENNY and HUMANITY cling together, scared.

MERDE: What's the scoop? Who's the sheila?
   Who's the shameless husband-stealer?

JENNY: I'm Jenny MacReddie, I'm Scotland the New,
   And who, may I ask, exactly are you?

The 4 IMPOSTERS draw round LORD MERDE in a phalanx:

S-DROOL: I, Charity, declare Lord Merde
   'Most Charitable Man I ever heard' –

S-SITCOM: And Love and Respect declares him elected
   The human being most loved and respected . . .

S-CARD: I worship him on bended knee
   For Services to Equality

R-DEN: Democracy's Award is won
   By News of the World, The Times, The Sun
   His stand at Wapping kept us free
   We say: Give him the BBC
   And Channel Four and ITV!
   I hereby rename Democracy
   In his honour – Merde-ocracy!

MERDE: Thank you, boys and girls, your jobs are secure
   (to audience) Until I throw them out the door –
   (to JENNY) Now, little girl, our plan's gone smoothly
   Now you roll up and bowl a googly:
   But I don't need no fortune-teller
   To know you'll never snitch this feller
   You both belong, – please make no fuss –
   Him to Gloria, you to us –

JENNY: I beg your pardon, 'belong to you'?
   No rougher wooing since to woo
   Came Henry's the Eighth to make Scotland his wife –
   He burnt down Embro, raped all Fife!

R-DENUN: Your will may be iron, defences stout:
   You'll never hope to keep him out!
   The world entire is quite emphatic —
   Democracy is Merde-ocratic:
   The Soviet Empire tottered, crumbled,
   Europe obeys him, happy to be humbled,
   All Asia receives by his satellite
   His news, his orders, day and night:
   Australia's his, America too:
   Can you resist, so small, so few?

S-SITCOM: **(to HUMANITY)** Humanity, dear King, dear groom,
   Come dress for your impending doom —
   Soon she'll be standing at your side,
   Your Gloria, your virgin bride . . .

They dress him as for a wedding.

JENNY is heart-broken.

MERDE: Now don't you fret, I'll see you right,
   I'll spread the word to all me mates,
   Just open your doors and strive to please
   The multinational companies
   You're mine, but I won't keep you to myself
   Just lie on your back, and think of the wealth —
   You work for them, your land won't spoil
   We've already taken most of your oil!

JENNY is heart-broken.

As HUMANITY is dressed in a consumerist wedding outfit by the IMPOSTERS, JENNY comes down and speaks to the WORTHY MOB — MUSIC behind

JENNY: To be born into the ending of this century
      When the heart must turn to stone to win the game,
   And the hardest thing to hold to's called Humanity,
      In a cruel world where no-one takes the blame,

   To be born into a century of nightmare
      Brutality and terror, ethnic hate
   Where a man will kill another for his pleasure
      And to suffer rape and torture is called fate:

   To be born into a world of greed and envy
      Where you grind your neighbour's face beneath your feet
   If you don't lie and cheat you're certain to go hungry,
      And you know you can't trust anyone you meet —

63

> We're abusing every child
> Who is born into this world
> For horror's waiting there
> In the dark below the stair:
> We're abusing every child
> Who is born into this world . . .

But from time to time we try to start again,
　　To make a world that's different from the old
Where Humanity can take the leading reign
　　And where Love Your Neighbour is the truth we hold,

Yes from time to time we try to start again
　　To make a land that values love and feeling –
Where Humanity can blossom, feel no pain,
　　And the wounds of this poor century start healing . . .

Scene 7

The Wedding Unconsumed

A brazen fanfare, klaxons, coarse merriment noises, as HUMANITY steps forward in his wedding attire, and LORD MERDE in hisbishop's cope and mitre prepares to officiate.

SMART-CARD is the curate, and SLAVERING-DROOL takes lots of flash photos, while TERRESTRIAL-MUNDANE and LORD TECHNOCRASS appear in morning coats as ushers.

JENNY is consoled by NANCY NOFIERTY and STRAIGHT-TALKING as they all watch. RIGHTEOUS-DENUNCIATION as Best Man leads HUMANITY in, and down centre to wait for the bride. A nervous pause. A horrible wedding march, and GLORIA comes in, upstage centre, grotesquely bridal and sexy, on the arm of SIR RIGHTEOUS DENUNCIATION with SAL-SITCOM as bridesmaid carrying the train.

GLORIA is handed over to HUMANITY, who looks deeply miserable. LORD MERDE takes control.

MERDE: Beloved brethren of the Fourth Estaite,
　　We've gathered here to celebrate
　　These nuptials, 'cos they just can't wait, –
　　This lecherous lad, this bitch on heat –
　　So quick, or they'll chaver in the street:
　　The lad's a bit soft, she'll harden him up,
　　Till drunk on the overflowing cup
　　He'll rip her bodice, tear off her panties,

And teach her the ways of the nineteen-nineties!
Enough of the pleasantries, long we've waited:
Is there any good reason this can't be consummated?

Piercing squeals from all over, cries of No! No! as the EIGHT DANCERS rush in and surround JENNY, all talking to her at the same time, excited.

General confusion. ALL try to decipher what is being said to JENNY. Eventually she gets the picture, and quietens them down. She steps out.

JENNY: Before we get to throwing the rice
I need to know on whose advice,
Humanity, you chose this woman?

MERDE: He chose himself – he's only human, –

R-DENUN: **(As Democracy)** It is. his democratic duty
To wed this stunning Page Three Beauty –

S-SITCOM: **(As Love & Respect)** And who are you, Miss Party-Pooper?
The jilted wife, as seen by Jilly Cooper!

S-DROOL: **(As Charity)** I, Charity, said Tie the Knot:
And Charity says . . . You should be shot!

S-CARD: **(As Equality)** Your moral tone, superior attitudes
Are nothing but non-egalitarian platitudes:
I suggest you exit to some colder latitudes!

HUMANITY: Jenny, these, my friends, advise
That I must wed the fair Cupsize –
I always listen when they speak,
Obey, for they are strong. I'm weak.
All down the years they've kept me safe,
And told me who to make my wife –
My poor wives die, they wither, fade:
My friends console me when they're dead,
Protect me, hide me, bring me bread.

JENNY: Then hear what my friends here have to report:
Postpone this wedding till you've heard and thought:
I asked them find me advisers true
To help us know what's best to do:
They have a tale; now hear it through!
Annie . . .

One of the DANCERS, ANNIE, steps out:

ANNIE: I went North-West, to the Hebrides.
And there in the Minch's storm-blown seas
The lonely isle of Handa stands
Where sea-birds screech on rocks and strands,

But there I spied a hermit's cell:
And as the wild waves roared and fell
I saw the face I longed to see:
The face of True Democracy.

HUMANITY is amazed, starts to speak, but JENNY silences him.

JENNY: Kirsti —

Another DANCER, KIRSTI, steps forward:

KIRSTI: Into the Northland I went, bold,
Through winters dark, and piercing cold,
Past towering crags, past nuclear domes
That light our streets, and rot our bones,
And there on top of the Stack of Hoy
I saw a sight filled me with joy:
Alone, in tears, but clear to see
Sat grieving, True Equality . . .

Again HUMANITY tries, but JENNY stops him.

JENNY: Mairi —

Another DANCER, MAIRI, steps forward.

MAIRI: Well I went West, to Mull, Tiree,
And searched the ever-changing sea,
Swam with the dolphins, soared with the eagle
Ransacked old tales of Finn and Fearghail,
Till at the tip of a point of Skye
Droukit, spent, despair in her eye,
There huddled the person I did not expect:
My guide, my star, Love and Respect —

HUMANITY: **(Bursts out)** I can't believe my ears, my eyes!

MERDE: Forget it — it's a pack of lies!

JENNY: Tanya

Another DANCER, TANYA, steps up.

TANYA: I went East, where Tantalon braves
The fierce North Sea and its grasping waves,
I scanned the coast, from Berwick to Wick
And saw not one man I would care to bring back:
And then, below, dying in a cave
The one I knew I'd come to save:
Oh yes, I love these other three:
But the greatest of all is Charity.

JENNY: Thank you, girls. It's the truth they tell,
    Lord Merde and his mates can go to hell,
    These vain, corrupt and devious twisters
    Are the Fourth Estaite's Quisling Imposters!

Uproar, the IMPOSTERS leap up and charge around attacking her, LORD MERDE, SIR TERRESTRIAL-MUNDANE, and LORD TECHNOCRASS go into conference, HUMANITY and GLORIA have a great row, and through it all, a beat, the DANCERS' feet tap out a figure that gets louder, and a fanfare sounds from all over the hall.

Scene 8

Re-Entry of the Gladiators

The re-entrance, in rags and plain shifts, of DEMOCRACY, EQUALITY, CHARITY, and LOVE & RESPECT.

The drums and the drumming of the feet rise, and the brass continues to blast out around the hall as they re-enter through the audience from four different corners, meet at one spot, then march together to the stage, shake HUMANITY'S hand, and JENNY's, then stare at the IMPOSTERS in their cloaks.

DEMOCRACY stops the noises with a gesture.

DEMOCRACY: Harry, dear friend, we came at speed
    To guard and defend you in your need,
    Only Democracy, Love, Equality
    And Charity can safeguard Humanity
    We left you alone, went North in fear,
    But we heard you're in danger, so we're here –

HUMANITY: But how – ? But what – ? But – **(points to IMPOSTERS)** who are these?
    They posed, pretended to advise,
    Paid for this wedding, cost a pretty penny – ?

BRAW BOB: It was a' to stop ye wenchin' wi' Jenny!

He moves onto the stage, with his MOB

    Tae let ye know, this bastard Merde,
    This floating raft of Aussie turd,
    Was scared young Jenny, if she wed
    Or took a decent man tae bed
    Would pay attention to her man

And on his media place a ban!
For me, I'd drap his troosers doon
And kick his erse frae toon tae toon
Then lower him slowly off Stranraer
Intae the pit where the old bombs are
But fill with lead each sweaty boot
In case some fisher fished him oot!
(Shrugs) But suit yersels –

He saunters back to join the MOB.

S-SITCOM: Such sacrilege I've never heard,
To speak like that of Bishop Lord Merde!

SIR R-DEN: This riff-raff boss, this Yahoo king,
This Prince of Scroungers should kneel, kiss his ring!

B-BOB: Away and kiss his ring yersel'
Ye've been daein' it for years, truth to tell –
Yer tongue's so brown yer words all smell . . .

S-CARD: This alchie scum-bag thinks he's Jesus –

S-DROOL: But horror, shock, he's rich as Croesus,
This Baron of the down-and-outs,
Runs drug-rings, pushers, pimps and touts,
Should be behind bars, out of the way:
(to BRAW BOB) So – shut the fuck up, or you're expose!

B-BOB: Come outside and say that and I'll feed traffic-meters wi' yer Willie in
2Op slices – and that's flattering ye

JENNY: Stop! Now I am the spirit of a land new born,
Not some nursery-rhyme maiden all forlorn –
It seems skulduggery's in the air
Before this land so new and fair
Has opened its doors, put up its sign:
So: what's the reason for this crime?
Imposters, speak. Just take your time . . .
Nancy, Straigh-Talking, control your fury –
You be the judges, the Worthy Mob the jury –

The IMPOSTERS form a line pushing the one at the front forward, but he or she just runs round the back until they reach the immovable bulk of BRAW BOB. He shunts the whole lot forward, and SMART-CARD finds himself on the spot.

NANCY: **(as Judge)** Name?

S-CARD: Bruce Bly Smart-Card

S-TALKING: **(as Judge)** Bly?

S-CARD: Me Dad hated rebels – so I conform
    He thought my name should also be Norm –
    But I had to have Bruce, *and* Bly – but see:
    It wouldn't be normal if I should have three!

S-TALKING: Place of Birth?

S-CARD: Under a slag-heap at Broken Hill
    Me mum gave birth: she lives there still,
    A simple dwelling, dusted with zinc,
    Leaning a bit, east, away from the stink – (Is ready to go on)

NANCY: Thank you. Occupation?

S-CARD: News Corpse Exec, Media Capo,
    UberGruppen Fuhrer in Merde's Gestapo,
    Something looks ripe, Lord Merde will buy it
    Then rocket me in to multiply it,
    He buys a paper, I sack the staff,
    Cut the price, run a lottery, make Merde laugh.
    And if our own boys, like sad Andrew Neil
    Don't cut it, can't make it, they're out, no appeal,
    See Kelvin, our hero, like Andrew was cocky –
    But both went to seed, like a twenty-stone jockey.
    In cable and Sky we're ahead of the game –
    We own satellites, decoders, all that you need,
    So you'll pay every which way our profits to feed.
    We bought movie studios, like Twentieth-Century Fox
    And we change our execs every day, like our socks,
    We make rubbish, but smartest, their libraries came –
    Millions of hours that all look the same:
    We pump them out nightly: and mix in some new ones
    Then really clean up with some sweet little blue ones . . .
    Got the picture?

S-TALKING: Oh aye, the picture's got quality:
    But why were you posing as him, as Equality?

S-CARD: Well nothing seems so wrong to me:
    I'm entitled to be called Equality
    To think I'm not is pure dim-witted.
    My defence is this: no crime was comitted!

NANCY: What's so equal about you and your kind?

S-TALKING: Is Venus equal to a cow's behind?

S-CARD: In this great democracy we all enjoy
    All men are equal, that you can't deny,
    Some must go first, like carts and horses –
    But that's the blessing of your Market Forces,

You know where you stand, – or sit – or lie –
But all have the right to take off, to fly!
Even, like us, to orbit the sky:
And when you recall my humble beginnings,
And see me now, counting my winnings,
A living proof my whole life gives:
The System works! Equality lives!

NANCY: Equality, step forward. Let us see
    Your claim to exclusivity –

EQUALITY: There's many came from poor beginnings,
    But few lay hands on such handsome winnings –
    We can't see life as a bookies' shop,
    As a lottery with the prize at the top
    And millions of hungry folk below,
    Powerless, voiceless, unable to grow: –

S-CARD: Such bleeding hearts can't be afforded –
    Surely effort must be rewarded!
    Lord Merde has brought in a revolution –
    Would he have bothered without motivation?
    Such men have built the British nation!
    Besides, we all have an equal vote –
    If any government gets our goat
    We can all put an x on their farewell note!

EQUALITY: Do you think all the voters in Gorgie, Dalry
    Weigh equal to the votes of the C.B.I.?
    Our votes aren't equal: that's a lie!
    If a poor man bothers his vote to cast
    His power has gone till five years have passed,
    If life's a horse-race, his came last!

S-CARD: There's no wrong British Justice can't restore:
    All men are equal before the Law!
    Our chances are the same, neither less nor more . . .

EQUALITY: Can any of them (the Mob) stand equally
    In the eyes of the law's great majesty
    With the directors of Guinness pic?
    Lord Merde's great wealth surrounds with a cloak
    Of privilege that works like smoke
    To screen his attacks, his bayonet charges.
    So no law can catch up with his devious urges,
    He flits from land to land, a grisly spectre,
    Red-toothed, uncaught, like Hannibal Lecter –
    But if in Britain he's caught cheating
    He buys smooth tongues and lawyers come bleating
    Who hunt the pages of old legal tomes,

Invent smart reasons to excuse his crimes
For massive fees ensure he's forgiven:
Such is Equality in the times we live in:
The law is by cash, not equality driven!

S-CARD: Bull-shit! Each one of these, like me,
Has an equal opportunity
To rise up the meritocracy!

EQUALITY: The chance to rise? Is Equal? Fair?
If a flea is equal to a grizzly bear . . .
While governments starve state education,
Eton survives: new leaders of the nation
Bald at twelve, gold in their veins,
For a nonchalant air they take great pains,
They're bred and trained to seize the reins:
Oh missus –
    Are their chances the same as your weans' ?

S-CARD: They all have equal rights to wealth
And life, and happiness and health!

EQUALITY: Of all the falseties you're propounding
That one is surely the most astounding!
In Britain now the only way
To health is to be rich enough to pay –
You're not so equal if you're poor –
Your hospitals closed, closed every door
Your doctors, nurses, porters fight –
But lose: for health's no more your right . . .
But happiness!? Aye, we can all be happy
If we've popped an E or sunk a drappie,
Or shot up crack or snorted a line:
Aye, happiness – for your kids, and mine.

S-CARD: You can't blame me, I didn't pervert them:
The parents are to blame: they spoil, then desert them –
Anyway, the kids of the aristocracy
Snort coke, smoke heroin, shoot crack, drop E:
Now that's what I call Equality.

NANCY: You stand condemned by your own foul word –
You're guilty – but sentence is deferred
For reports from a psycho-analyst
Who'll probably say you're round the twist.

S-CARD: Oh no – *they* **(audience)** all think just like me –
That we live in an equal society . . .

S-TALKING: I can't believe they've all gone crazy –

NANCY: No but quite a few's gone soft or hazy –

S-TALKING: Call the next prisoner. We suspect
 She'll claim she's the genuine Love and Respect!

S-TALKING: Name?

S-SITCOM: Sally Sitcom, aka Sal Soaps –

NANCY: **(Reads)** You stand accused of dangling false hopes,
 Polluting with violence the minds of the young,
 And peddling false values you know to be wrong.

S-TALKING: Occupation?

S-SITCOM: I go to market to choose for you
 The soaps and series you'll pay to view,
 If you want guns and violent death
 I'll buy stuff to take away your breath,
 If you want teenage tears and gushes
 You've got it, you want mid-life hot flushes,
 Big business drama, tycoons and power
 I'll feed you your dosage, for hour after hour,
 But cops, and psycho killers grab
 The ratings for us, they're just fab!
 I buy in bulk at rock-bottom prices
 But must get ratings or there'll be a crisis,
 Lord Merde and his eagle-eye will spot it
 And Smart-Card in the neck will get it,
 The only cause for which they care
 Is the cause for the dip in the audience share:
 Our job's not programmes, we're not cultural advisers,
 But to sell a big audience to rich advertisers
 So I must grab 'em, by sex, gun or shlock
 From six in the morning round the clock –
 And if! don't, you'll hear them cry:
 You're out, Ms Sitcom, – Bye, Bye-bye!

S-TALKING: So what made you think, I mean how d'you expect
 The world to accept you as Love and Respect?

S-SITCOM: These days our communal instinct's low,
 Extended families we just don't know,
 So the young watch soaps to learn to grow:
 Their social self, their group behaviour's
 Learnt from Home and Away, and Neighbours,
 Or Californians with padded crutch,
 Desporting their bodies in Baywatch –
 And so they learn what True Love means,
 Those dear, confused, impressionable teens!
 As for Respect, that's for Authority

That's male, and white, and sixty-three:
All this and more they learn from me:
The young today just don't connect
With her ancient ideas of Love and Respect –

STRAIGHT-TALKING, NANCY NOFIERTY and all turn to the real LOVE & RESPECT, who rises, shaky.

L&R: A lot of what you say is true:
    The crime is surely what you do
    To sell some roots to a rootless child,
    To simulate love in a loveless world;
    In America now their Deity
    Is a deep, complete Hypocrisy,
    Their God is their Image, their Hell is Reality,
    Which must be concealed, so, wreathed in smiles,
    Tycoons can push up their global sales,
    The blacks, the abusers, the urban poor
    Are invisible to them, locked the door,
    And you, (Sal) and your master's occupation
    Is to profit by building their self-delusion,
    And now you're paid a mighty fee
    To fill the whole world with hypocrisy,
    And the lies of your fantasy factory.

S-SITCOM: You kill-joy, puritan, punitive elitist,
    They love to dream – and our dreams are the sweetest:
    What matters isn't the harsh, the real,
    But the way that simple people feel:
    If they feel good, that's great: what's wrong?
    We can't all want to grow up, be strong!

L&R: Respect is first for the lives of others
    To feel for all like sisters, brothers,
    Their bodies, minds, their gender, faith,
    Their difference, their separate truth:
    The others you show are things to kill,
    The Media's Triumph of the Will,
    Where nightly all problems' resolution
    Is shoot-outs: the fantasy Final Solution:
    If that's what it takes to make them feel good,
    The world grows sicker, mankind's gone mad.

S-SITCOM: Oh it's only meant to entertain!
    There's always someone to complain –
    They're none too bright, their lives are dull,
    They need adventure, the vicarious thrill!

L&R: Their intelligence can't be neglected,
    Their right to think must be respected,

Their imagination, their culture, dreams
Deserve respect:

S-SITCOM: That's not how it seems
To us, you naive, would-be Goebels:
Its market-research, not do-gooder's fables
That teach us what to buy and show:
They **love** our programmes, **(To audience)** is that not so?

L&R: Ah love, yes love; true love must be
The seed-bed of Humanity,
The soil where all true feeling grows,
Love is the stem: Peace is the rose.
But love can't come from sentiment or slush,
It quickly dies when fed on gush,
And love's not screwing or he-man rape,
Submission, lust or clumsy grope:
The feet of love are on the ground –
It sees more clearly, hears the sounds
Of life and death and constancy:
Without it, humans, can't be free . . .

S-SITCOM: What high-falutin' crap you spout,
You and your kind should be driven out,
My colleague Dickie Slavering-Drool
Will sort you out, you prissy fool,
Sir Righteous will denounce you thundering,
Call you a Marxist, a Red, a blundering
Moralist, from Mars we must suspect
Of corrupting minors: you're not Love and Respect!

NANCY: Enough! You've blown it! Guilty as hell!
Imposter, Fraud, and Ne'er-Do-Well!
Next prisoner!

S-TALKING: **(to R-DENUN)** Name, and Occupation –

R-DEN: I am Sir Righteous Denunciation.
I buy and sell antiques and books –
My charming accent, my schoolboy looks
Got me a job on a right-wing paper,
I studied the City and praise Mrs Thatcher –
The greatest leader that ever there's been,
In my opinion she'd make a great queen,
Her strictures strict, her orders clear
Filled me, like Nanny's, with a thrilling fear:
I applauded her lofty morality
So she put me in charge of the BBC,
I praised her disdain for bleeding hearts,
So she gave me the Council of the Arts,

I mucked out that stable, routed the lot,
Gave those woofters and arties one hell of a shot,
Closed half of them down, their 'art' was all rot,
These Marxists and lefties are Nazis, accursed,
Or that's what they taught me at Stonyhurst –
Mrs T was delighted, with pride I just burst;
She made me Chief Censor for British TV,
Though they censored themselves more completely than me:
Like being a dentist to a man with no teeth!
I basked in the shade of the puritan Reith:
But poor Margaret went mad, gibbering, barking,
And alas, poor me, I had to start working:
I write a column that roars like thunder
Defends the right to exploit and plunder –
Makes these lefties stop and wonder:
This world is moving, – and I'm proud, so darn it! –
A lot to the right of Alfred Lord Garnett!

S-TALKING: So why Democracy? What's your excuse
     For posing as something you think is no use!

R-DEN: Au contraire, I'm democratic!
     Give or take a few skeletons in the attic.
     My point is this: Man must be free
     To practise this democracy –
     Free to buy, free to sell, in an open market,
     Free to make profit and free to take it
     Free of interference from the state,
     No communist tax to de-motivate.
     Life's losers ? Well – they're free to meet their fate:
     Yes freedom is needed for the strong to rise
     For power to the powerful, control to the wise
     Domination to the rich and no compromise!

DEMOCRACY: If that's your Democracy, I rest my case:
     You're a walking scab, a deep disgrace:
     This freedom's no friend to Democracy.
     For we all have the responsibility
     To make this world a better place
     For all the members of the human race,
     And freedom is never unconfined:
     We are not free to trick and bind
     The poor, the weak, to rob the blind
     We are constrained by many a tether
     If we may happily live together,
     Freedom is relative, happily,
     For all to live in society . . .

R-DEN: Marxist! Trot! Nazi swine!

Democracy is mine to define!
I'll shut you up, on stage, on screen,
Your propaganda won't be heard or seen!
Disloyal! Totalitarian Slave! Obscene!

He begins to pummell DEMOCRACY, and is restrained by STRAIGHT-TALKING

NANCY: That's quite enough! Sit down, relax –

DEMOCRACY: You've sold your soul for a cut in tax!
    Like your heroine Thatcher, you sometimes reveal
    The greed your dogma tries to conceal,
    The hollow simper, the viper's eyes
    Can't hide the fact you both despise
    The weak, the old, the sick, the poor
    For whom you piously pretend to care –
    Freedom's a word you stole from me,
    The most abused of words is: Free.

S-TALKING: **(to R-DEN)** Sit there, and contemplate your crimes –
    You can aye attack us in the Sunday Times!

NANCY: Now last, who's this?

S-DROOL: I'm Slavering Drool,
    A humble accessory, Lord Merde's poor tool,
    I've done no harm, just done my job,
    Wrote a few words, earned a few bob:
    If Charity is not me but she,
    Then Charity's what you should be showing to me:
    I'm a wage-slave, wi' three kids, a wife –
    One day I hope I'll get a life
    But till that day, I do as I'm bid –
    No more than anyone ever did.

NANCY: What did you do? Your occupation,
    And why you claim our approbation.

S-DROOL: Oh no, I don't expect approval –
    Just, please, no quick unfair dismissal,
    I'm not a hero, a saint, or a hostage,
    I'm just a pile of natural wastage.

NANCY: Your job?

S-DROOL: My job? Oh this and that,
    Mostly reporting, show-biz chat,
    I exposed Bill Connolly, stopped him joking, –
    I told his wife who he'd been poking,
    I found an MP in bed with another,

A story the cabinet failed to smother,
A soap-star's fellatio I exposed,
And a palace door open, that should have been closed,
I bought the exclusive to the Squidgy tape
And snapped Diana improving her shape,
Now Gordon Brown . . . I'm sniffing around –
Why's he no' marrit? The truth I'll find!
If only Tony Blair was gay
I'd crucify him every day
And sell, before the story'd run,
A billion copies of The Sun –
Don't get me wrong, I'm Labour, me:
I'd have to do it, I'm a professional, see,
But jings I'd come in for a mighty fee –
And then I could retire, a winner,
And take the wife out for her dinner,
A bungalow on Arran wi' a garden:
That's all I want. A Royal Pardon.

S-TALKING: God what a creep – so, Charity,
Will you put him out of his misery?

CHARITY: The best can be said for Slavering-Drool
Is, I'm afraid, he's a sleazy fool:
The lies he's told, the cruel distortion,
The prejudice fed, pure sensation's
The excuse for criminal trivialisation,
And then there's war, when war-lord Thatcher
Sank the wrong boat, his headline: Gotcha!
His patriotic fervour smells,
But that's what a tabloid cynically sells:
Iraqis, Argies, Colonel Gadafi,
Arafat last year, this year still a bit iffy,
Micks and Teagues and Gerry Adams,
Whose smile's more deadly even than Saddam's,
Scroungers in luxury on the dole,
Miners whose jobs their campaign stole,
Blacks with mythical drugs and powers,
Asians who take what's rightly ours,
These and so many they fear, despise,
He's happy to turn on, to demonise,
Oh Charity's stretched to forgive this twister –
But it all leads back to his Lord and Master
Perhaps his life's more chance to be spared
If we put in the dock the great Lord Merde . . .

NANCY: D'you think?

JENNY: Ida If he contrives

To buy up Scotland, all our lives
Are put at risk of terminal Deceit,
Corrupt reporting will defeat
Our democratic hopes, capsize
Our boat in trivialities and lies.
If he comes in, these creeps come too,
Humanity goes – and so do you:
No longer the Scotland that we desire,
But a profit-stream for a crook and a liar!

NANCY: Then call Lord Merde, into the dock –

S-TALKING: Call Lord Merde, call Lord Merde – och!

MERDE: You can't do that! Contact my Solicitor –
I'm not a Brit, I'm just a visitor,
I'm not responsible, don't shoot the messenger,
These people here, Scots, Brits, whatever
Demand what we sell: so we'll sell it forever!
I'm not a crook, I'm an entrepreneur
My head in the clouds, my feet in the sewer,
I'm a businessman, mate, just better than most:
They'd all do the same if they'd thought of it first
So piss off to Messrs D.Lay and X.Pense,
They're paid to protect me from noxious offence, –
I haven't got time to sit here all night,
I'm launching a digital satellite!

LORD T: Hear Hear! You simply can't see, you are blind
To his great contribution to the wealth of mankind,
You see progress demands expensive research
So he needs to get richer to carry the torch
Of science, technology on through the years –

MERDE: Thanks Technocrass, mate, here, get in some beers –

SIR T-M: Lord Merde's a broadcaster, not just a slob:
(And the way things are going he'll provide my next job)
How dare you suggest you'll refuse him admission
Will not Freedom of Speech be in your Constitution?

LORD T: Technology rules, that's what it's about,
And Technology says: You can't keep him out!

SIR T-M: With the Scottish Sun, and the dish and the cable
His feet are already under your table.

LORD T: He'll bring you investment, lots of employment,
And movies and fabulous future enjoyment.
You must let him in, he's progress embodied, –

SIR T-M: You can't keep him out, your nose will be bloodied

MERDE: Thanks, boys, now we're off, Gloria, wake up!
  (to JENNY) You're on to a loser, give yourself a shake-up:
  I've mates in the government and the opposition,
  In Europe, – in the parliament and the Commission –
  I've mates in high places all round the globe,
  I've the slyness of Eve, the patience of Job,
  And no-one denies me, no-one tries me,
  I'll change your Assembly till it satisfies me:
  But this Westminster Government
  Gives more and more of what we want
  Our power grows, they give more yet,
  We buy more papers, TV stations,
  More satellites, till all the nations
  Of the world are on our list:
  Scotland won't dare, it can't resist:
  For I, McDonalds and the CIA
  Are masters of the world today:
  Without us, shame! For we, you see
  Are symbols of Democracy –
  So open your doors, to us, be free –
  Or goodbye your prosperity!
  Come boys and girls, we're off to China:
  Our foot's in the door, so nothing could be finer!

LORDS MERDE and TECHNOCRASS, SIR TERRESTRIAL-MUNDANE and SIR RIGHTEOUS DENUNCIATION, SLAVERING-DROOL, SAL SITCOM and SMART-CARD all form up to make a big exit. GLORIA is reluctant to leave.

Then as Amazing Grace is starting up, a figure appears at the back of the hall GRANPA JOCK. He yells:

G-JOCK: Stop! Don't let them go, not yet!
  There's a thing they're trying to forget!
  In the years since 1984
  Ye made one hundred and eighty billion pounds or more,
  Profit with forty per cent tax to pay,
  Since you made it in the good old UK:
  So far what have you paid? Not 2 per cent,
  If we dinnae pay tax, tae jail we're sent:
  So seventy-five billion pounds you're owing,
  One-tenth to Scotland to get us going:
  Seven and a half billion pounds, if you please,
  Or into Saughton wi' the rats and the fleas.

MERDE: My tax is paid, it's all above board,
  Your government gave its solemn word
  That if I invested, brought jobs and cash,
  Supported their efforts the unions to bash,
  Rubbished Neil Kinnock, and student-protesters,

> They'd favour my Corp. and my US investors,
> The tax-rate in Britain had no need to alarm us:
> We'd take profits tax-free in the far-off Bahamas!

G-JOCK: What a wonderful deal – Shock horror, Sensational!

MERDE: It's the same as the average multi-national,
  The guys who take oil from the stormy North Sea
  Pay even less tax to your country than me!
  Off our cake you can't take the marzipan and icing,
  So we dreamt up a system we call transfer-pricing!
  It's all a bit legal, so we're hunky-dory –

G-JOCK: No wonder The Sun and the Times scream: Vote Tory.

MERDE: So out of our way, you failed debt-collector,
  You'll need to employ a new tax-inspector,
  But mark my words: if Scotland tries
  To tax Multi-Nationals, Scotland dies!
  We're each of us bigger and richer than you:
  We'll sod off to Spain, and leave you in the stew!

He gestures, *Amazing Grace* plays, and they sweep out through the audience, boo-ed by the MOB.

Scene 9

Resolution and Independence

STRAIGHT-TALKING and NANCY NO-FIERTY move down, speak to the audience:

S-TALKING: So much for justice in the Global Village,
  The strong have the right to rob and to pillage,
  Like war-lords in China, Mafiosi in Sicily,
  The old English barons, or Japanese Samurai
  They're licensed to kill, to exploit, to rip off:

NANCY: How can Jenny survive with those feet in her trough?

JENNY: I'll survive, don't fret: I can aye sing a song –
  It'll make us feel better, –

G-JOCK: But will no right a wrong!
  What hope from the other Estaites we have here,
  The Merchants, Lords Temporal and Spiritual appear
  To have fallen asleep or anyway impotent
  To deal with Lord Merde. Are they really so incompetent?

He examines the MERCHANTS:

> Low-Taxes, Cheap Labour, no chance, I'm sure,
> Their taxes not low enough, Labour too dear
> Send them off, they're no use to Scotland the New,
> They're Thatcher's bastards, not even true blue!

They are carried off to the applause of the MOB.

> Now Privatised Cedric, you're grinning a lot:
> But you'll never survive to control what you've got:
> For just when your joy overfloweth your cup –
> Some grey multinational will gobble you up!
> Take him off, he's no use, lead him to the slaughter:
> Let Scotland herself own her power and her water!

CEDRIC is carted off.

> Now the Second Estaite – those that no-one elected,
> Who rule our lives, obeyed, not respected,
> Lords Temporal, cocks on your dunghill crowing,
> Help us out, if you can, if not, get going!

He goes up to OVERLORD GLOBAL.

> Now here's a fine figure, it's Overlord Global –
> A fat multinational looking for trouble!
> In Scotland he'll try any scam to double
> His profits and grow till he pops like a bubble –
> He's no help against Merde, the problem's the same:
> If we try to control him, he'll go – that's his game!

Goes to JUMP-JET of NATO.

> Ah General Jump-Jet, the NATO commander,
> With the biggest army since Great Alexander,
> No help from you – you're a gun for hire:
> Oh they won't pay you now, but when you retire!

Moves to DUADIHL BACKHANDER

> But Duadihl Backhander, our only hope,
> Scotland in Europe, King Billy meets the Pope!
> We've given you powers to guard and proect us,
> To quarantine the dogs who come to infect us,
> But rabies is rampant, strange to relate:
> Have we set a mad dog to guard our own gate?
> Away with the lairds of the Second Estaite –

The Big-heads are taken off.

> Let's turn to the First, these Objects of Piety –

Margaret who sees no such thing as Society,
She closed down Scots industry, pits and steel,
Foul-hooked us and played us, Tight line, screaming reel,
Though we voted to sack her, she's what we got:
Sanctimonious, cruel, the scourge of the Scot.

Moves to John's statue:

John the Apologist, grey with worry,
Always seems to have come to say he's sorry, –
He's a lot to be sorry for: under his smile
Beats a heart of lead, Thatcher without style,
To cut the taxes of the owners of wealth
He's chopping away at our National Health,
To keep the rich in cars and yachts
He's killing our Welfare with a million cuts,
To stay in power he's dealt away
The chance for peace with the IRA,
To stay in power, his one obsession,
He's mortgaged our future for reposession,
He'll leave us cleaned out, with negative equity –
And call it a triumph of caution and gravity.

Moves to BLAIR:

Behold our saviour, Blair of Galilee
Who will rise again if he gives us an Assemblily
If he gave us a government we'd chant his praise,
He'd ascend into heaven after forty days!
But his plans to make Labour middle-class
He can keep in England: they shall not pass,
Return to sender, Pontius Pilate,
Who slew the first-born, nothing to smile at . . .
Was it Pilate who taught him to wash his hands
Of the unemployed and the workers, his truest friends:
In Scotland these of all people must be heard –
To take power from the poor is not to have cared:
New Labour can't mean just benevolent old laird!
So thanks if you midwife the birth of my Jenny,
Then leave us alone: our problems are many,
Go sort out poor England, it needs a good shake,
But let us get on, we've our future to make.

Points to statues of THATCHER and MAJOR.

So take away her, and take him to the zoo,
Put him (BLAIR) in the corner till we see what he'll do!

Looks round at the bare hillside

That's better, that's braw, this bonnie hillside
Is perfect for you, Sir, **(HUMANITY)** to make her your bride –

JENNY: This image of wedding is one from the past:
We know what you mean, a love that will last,
But marriage bonds are out this year:
We'll stick together, but not from fear
Of breaking vows or social stigma:
To love, we must be free: eternal enigma.

HUMANITY: **(sings)** Jenny, my dear, I'll love you till
The ocean rises above the hill –
But the ozone layer is crumbling still
So someday soon I know the hill will

JENNY: **(sing)** My darling man I do love you,
I'll love you till the moon turns blue –
But with pollution, radiation too,
The moon will soon have a blue-ish hue!

HUMANITY: **(sings)** I love you love till pigs do fly
And we all believe sty in the sky –
But wing implants need pigs to try,
So before very long they'll be fluttering by!

JENNY: **(sings)** My love is like a red red rose
That in a summer garden grows –
But when the wintry east wind blows
My petals will all fall as I blow my nose!

HUM & JEN: **(sing)** We're in agreement, there's no dissent:
To see what the weather and our luck has sent,
And if it seems our love's not spent,
We'll move in together and we'll save some rent –

HUMANITY: Yes if she stays true –

JENNY: And if he's not bent,
I'll take him to bed till our love is spent

HUMANITY: If we feel the same

JENNY: Then we know it's meant

BOTH: Then we'll hang out together and be quite content!

End of Song

S-TALKING: No wedding! How will we end the show?

NANCY: These young people today! I really don't know

LOVE & RESPECT, DEMOCRACY, EQUALITY and CHARITY gather round them:

L&R: As a non-wedding gift you can't reject
    I give, for each other, lifelong Respect –

CHARITY: At this un-matrimony, I Charity give
    The joy of helping others to live –

EQUALITY: Equality gives equality, each with other,
    Brother with sister, lover with lover –

DEMOCRACY: And I, Democracy, will to you
    The right to democracy, real and true

G-JOCK: Och I'm so happy! A lovely picture:
    I'll give them the whole of our Scottish culture,
    The songs, the stories, the way we cook,
    The schoolyard lore ye won't find in a book,
    The poems in Scots, in Gaelic, in Doric,
    The saddest tunes, the melodies euphoric,
    The patient pause, the time to think,
    The speediest wit, quick as a wink,
    And most of all, I set you free
    To move on from auld fools the like of me:
    On your way, do your worst, but make it your own –
    And then you've come of age: you've grown.

**Quiet music for the non-nuptials. They form a wedding group – BRAW BOB
comes to take the photo: he turns to the audience:**

B-BOB: All children need mums and dads to admire –
    And we, like you, have been daein' that here:
    But come the day the real thing starts
    We'll no' be just watchin', we'll be playing our parts –
    Till then, be patient, take your ease:
    (to GROUP) Hold still! Now smile! Say Scottish Cheese!

ALL: **(Smiling)** Scottish Cheese!

**BIG MUSIC, and the DANCERS come on and dance, the MOB fire streamers,
bells ring out and out of the merriment comes a Walk-Down, including
MERDE and the IMPOSTERS.**

The End

ANE SATYRE OF THE THRIE ESTAITES

Ane pleasant satyre or the thrie estaites in commendation
of vertew and vituperatioun of vyce, as followis.

DILIGENCE: The Father and founder of faith and felicitie,
    That your fassioun formed to his similitude
    And his Sone our Sauiour scheild in necessitie,
    That bocht yow from baillis ranson rude,
    Repleadge and his presonaris with his hart-blude
    The halie Gaist gouernour and grounder of grace
    Of wisdome and weilfair baith fontaine and flude,
    Gif yow all that I sie seasit in this place,
    And scheild yow from sinne.
    And with his Spreit yow inspyre
    Till I haue shawin my desyre
    Silence Soueraine I requyre
    For now I begin,

    Tak tent to me my freinds and hald yow coy,
    For I am sent to yow as messingeir,
    From ane nobill and rycht redoubtit Roy:
    The quhilk hes bene absent this monie yeir.

    Humanitie giue ye his name wald speir:
    Quha bade me shaw to yow but variance,
    That he intendis amang yow to compeir,
    With ane triumph and awfull ordinance:
    With crown and sword and scepter in his hand,
    Temperit with mercie quhen penitence appeiris:
    Howbeit that hee lang tyme hes bene sleipand,
    Quhairthrow misreull hes rung thir monie yeiris:
    That innocentis hes bene brocht on thair beiris,
    Be fals reporteris of this natioun:
    Thocht young oppressouris at the elder leiris,
    Be now assurit of reformatioun.

    Sie no misdoeris be sa bauld,
    As to remaine into this hauld:
    For quhy be him that Iudas sauld
    Thay will be heich hang it.

    Now faithfull folk for ioy may sing:
    For quhy it is the iust bidding
    Of my soveraine lord the king
    That na man be wrangit.

    Thocht he ane quhyll into his flouris
    Be gouernit be vylde trompouris:
    And sumtyme lufe his paramouris,
    Hauld ye him excusit.

    For quhen he meittis with Correctioun,
    With Veritie and Discretioun,
    Thay will be banisched aff the toun,
    Quhilk hes him abusit.

And heir be oppin proclamatioun,
I wairne in name of his magnificence,
The thrie estaitis of this natioun,
That thay compeir with detfull diligence?

And till his grace mak thair obedience.
And first I wairne the Spritualitie,
And sie the burgessis spair not for expence:
Bot speid thame heir with Temporalitie.

Als I beseik yow famous auditouris,
Conveinit in this congregatioun,
To be patient the space of certaine houris,
Till ye haue hard our short narratioun.

And als we mak yow supplicatioun,
That na man tak our wordis intill disdaine:
Althocht ye hear be declamatioun,
The common-weill richt pitiouslie complaine.

Rycht so the verteous ladie Veritie,
Will mak ane pitious lamentatioun:
Als for the treuth sho will impresonit be,
And banischit lang tyme out of the toun:

And Chastitie will mak narratioun,
How sho can get na ludging in this land,
Till that the heauinlie king Correctioun,
Meit with the king and commoun hand for hand.

Prudent peopill I pray yow all,
Tak na man greif in speciall:
For wee sall speik in generall,
For pastyme and for play.

Thairfoir till all our rymis berung,
And our mistoinit sangis be sung,
Leteuerie man keip weill ane toung,
And euerie woman tway.

Rex Humanitas
O Lord of Lords and King of kingis all,
Omnipotent of power Prince but peir,
Euer ringand in gloir Celestial
Quha be great micht and haising na mateir
Maid heauin and eird, fyre, air and watter cleir:
Send me thy grace with peace perpetuall,
That I may rewll my realme to thy pleaseir,
Syne bring my saull to ioy angelicall.
Sen thow hes giuin mee dominatioun

And rewll of pepill subiect to my cure,
Be I nocht rewlit be counsall and ressoun,
In dignitie I may nocht lang indure.
I grant mystait my self may nocht assure
Nor yit conserue my lyfe in sickernes:
Haue pitie Lord on mee thy creature
Supportand me in all my busines.
I thee requeist quha rent was on the Rude,
Me to defend from the deids of defame:
That my pepill report of mebot gude,
And be my saifgaird baith from sin and shame·
I knaw my day is induris bot as ane dreame,
Thairfoir O Lord I hairtlie the exhort,
To gif me grace to use my diadeame
To thy pleasure and to my great comfort.
Wantonnes.

WANTONNES: My Soueraine Lord and Prince but peir,
    Quhat garris yow mak sic dreirie cheir,
    Be blyth sa lang as year heir,
    And pas tyme with pleasure:

    For als lang leifis the mirrie man,
    As the sorie for ocht he can:
    His banis full sair Sir sall I ban
    That dois yow displeasure.

    Sa lang as Placebo and I,
    Remaines into your company,
    Your grace sall leif richt mirrely:
    Of this haif ye na dout.

    Sa lang as ye haue us in cure,
    Your grace sir sall want na pleasure:
    War Solace heir I yow assure,
    He wald reioyce this rout.

PLACEBO: Gude brother myne quhair is Solace
    The mirrour of all mirrines,
    I haue great meruell be the Mes
    He taries sa lang.
    Byde he away wee ar bot shent,
    I ferlie how he fra us went:
    I trow he hes impediment
    That lettis him nocht gang.

WANTONNES: I left Solace that same greit loun
    Drinkand into the burrows toun,
    It will cost him halfe of ane croun,
    Althocht he had na mair.

And als he said hee wald gang see Fair ladie Sensualltie,
The buriall of all bewtie
And portratour preclair.

PLACEBO: Be God I see him at the last
As he war chaist rynnand richt fast,
He glowris euin as he war agast
Or fleyit of ane gaist.

Na, he is wod drunkin I trow,
Se ye not that he is wod fow:
I ken weill be his creischie mow
He hes bene at ane feast.

SOLACE: Now quha saw euer sic ane thrang?
Me thocht sum said I had gaine wrang,
Had I help I wald sing ane sang
With ane rycht mirrie noyse.

I haue sic pleasour at my hart,
That garris me sing the troubill pairt:
Waldsum gude fallow sill the quart
It wald my hairt reioyce.

Howbelt my coat be short and nippit,
Thankis be to God I am weill hlpplt
Thocht all my gold may shone be grippit
Intill ane pennle pursse.

Thocht I ane seruand Jang haif bene,
My purchais Is nocht worth ane preine:
I may sing Peblis on the greine
For ocht that I may tursse.

Quhat is my name can ye not gesse,
Sirs ken ye nocht Sandie solace?
Thay callit my mother bonie Besse
That dwelt betwene the bowis.

Of twelf yeir auld sho learnit to swyfe,
Thankit be the great God on lyue:
Scho maid me fatheris four or fyue,
But dout this is na mowis.

Quhen ane was deid sho gat ane uther,
Was never man had sic ane mother:
Of fatheris sho maid me ane futher,
Of law it men and leirit:

Scho is baith wyse, worthie and wicht,
For scho spairis nouther kuik nor knycht:
Yea four and twentie on ane nicht,
And ay thair eine schobleirit,

And gif I lie sirs ye may speir:
Bot saw ye nocht the King cum heir?
I am ane sportour and playfeir
To that Royall young King:

He said he wald within schort space
Cum pas his tyme into this place:
I pray the Lord to send him grace,
That he lang tyme may ring.

PLACEBO: Solace quhy taryit ye sa lang?

SOLACE: The felnd a faster I micht gang:
I micht not thrlst out throw the thrang,
Of wyfes fyftein fidden
Then for to rln I tuik ane rink,
Bot I felt neuer sik ane stink:
For our lordis luif gif me ane drink,
Placebo my deir brother.

REX: My servant Solace quhat gart yow tarie?

SOLACE: I wait not sir be sweit saint Marie,
I haue bene in ane feirie farie
Or ellis intill ane trance:

Sir I haue sene I yow assure
The fairest earthlie creature,
That ever was formit be nature
And maist for to advance –

To luik on hir is great delyte,
With lippis reid and cheikis quhyte
I wald renunce all this warld quyte
For till stand in hir grace:

Scho is wantoun and scho is wyse:
And cled scho is on the new gyse,
It wald garall your flesche up ryse
To luik upon hir face.

War I ane king it sould be kend,
I sould not spair on hir to spend:
And this same nicht for hir to send,
For my pleasure:

Quhat rak of your prosperities
Gif ye want Sensualitie?
I wald nocht gif ane sillie file,
For your treasure.

REX: Forsufth my frelnds I think ye ar not wyse,

Till counsall me to break commandement
Directit be the Prince of Paradyce:
Considering ye knaw that my intent
Is for till be to God obedient,
Quhilk dois forbid men to be lecherous:
Do I nocht sa perchance I will repent,
Thairfoir I think your counsall odious
The quhilk ye gaif mee till.
Becaus I haue bene to this day
Tanquam tabula rasa:

That is als mekill as to say.
Redie for gude and ill.

PLACEBO: Beleiue ye that we will begyll yow,
Or from your vertew we will wyle yow,
Or with euill counsall overseyll yow,
Both into gude and euill:

To tak your graces part wee grant
In all your deidis participant,
Sa that ye be nocht ane young sanct
And syne ane auld deuill.

WANTONNES: Beleiue ye Sir that Lecherie be sin,
Na, trow nocht that, this is my ressoun quhy,
First at the Romance Kirk will ye begin
Quhilk is the lemand lamp of lechery:
Quhair Cardinals and Bischops generally
To luif Ladies thay think ane pleasant sport,
And out of Rome hes baneist Chastity
Quha with our Prelats can get na resort,

SOLACE: Sir quhill ye get ane prudent Queine,
I think your Maiestie serein
Sould haue ane lustie Concubein,
To play yow withall:

For I knaw be your qualitie.
Ye want the gift of chastitie
Fall to *in nomine Domini,*
This is my counsall.

I speik Sir under protestatioun,
That nane at me haif indignatioun:
For all the Prelats of this natioun,
For the maist part:

Thay think na schame to haue ane huir,
And sum hes thrie under thair cuir:
This to be trew He yow assuir
Ye sall heir efterwart.

Sir knew all the mater throch
To play ye wald begin
Speir at the Monks of Bamirrinoch,
Giflecherie be sin.

PLACEBO: Sir send ye for Sandie solace
Orells your monyeoun Wantonnes,
And pray my Ladie Priores,
The suith till declair:

Gif it be sin to tak Kaity,
Or to leif like ane bummill baty
The buik sayis *Omnia probate*
And nocht for to spair.

SENSUALITIE: Luifers awalk behald the fyrie spheir,
Behauld the naturall dochter of Venus:
Behauld luifers this lustie Ladie cleir
The fresche fonteine of Knichtis amorous
Repleit with joyis duice and delicious
Or quha wald mak to Venus observance.
In my mirthfull chalmer melodious?
Thair sall thay find all pastyme and pleasance
Behauld my heid behauld my gay attyre,
Behauld my halse lusum and lilie quhite:
Behauld my visage flammand as the fyre
Behauld my papis of portratour perfyte.
To luke on mee lufferis hes greit delyte,
Rycht sa hes all the Kinges of Christindome:
To thame I haif done pleasouris infinite,
And speciallie unto the Court of Rome.
Ane kis of me war worth in ane morning
A milyioun of gold to Knicht or King.
And yit I am of nature sa towart
I lat no luiffer pas with ane sair hart.
Of my name wald ye wit the veritie,
Forsuith thay call me Sensualitie.
I hauld it best now or we farther gang,
To Dame Venus let vs go sing ane sang.

HAMLINES: Madame but tarying,
For to serue Venus deir,
We sall fall to and sing,
Sister Danger cum neir.

DANGER. Sister I was nocht sweir
To Venus observance,
Howbeit I mak Dangeir:
Yit be continuance,
Men may haue thair pleasance:

93

Thairfoir let na man fray,
We will tak it perchance,
Howbeit that wee say nay.

HAMELINES: Sister cum on your way,
And let us nocht think lang:
In all the haist wee may,
To sing Venus ane sang.

DANGER: Sister sing this sang I may not,
Without the help of gude Fund-Jonet:
Fund-Jonet, hoaw cum tak a part.

FUND-JONET: That sall I do with all my hart:
Sister howbeit that I am hais,
I am content to beir a bais.
Ye twa sould luif me as your lyfe,
Ye knaw I lernit yow baith to swyfe:
In my chalmer ye wait weill quhair,
Sen syne the feind ane man ye spair.

HAMELINES: Fund-Jonet, fy, ye ar to blame,
To speik foull wordis think ye not schame?

FUND-JONET: Thair is ane hundreth heir sitand by
That luifis geaping ais weill as I,
Micht thay get it in priuitie:
Bot quha begins the sang let se.

REX: Up Wantonnes thow sleipis to lang,
Me thocht I hard ane mirrie sang:
I the command in haist to gang
Se quhat yon mirth may meine.

WANTONNES: I trow Sir be the Trinitie
Yon same is Sensualitie,
Gif it be scho sune sall I sie
That Soverance sereine.

REX: Quhat war thay yon to me declair?

WANTONNES: Dame Sensuall baith gude and fair.

PLACEBO: Sir scho is mekill to avance,
For scho can baith play and dance:
That perfyt patron of plesance
Ane perle of pulchritude:
Soft as the silk is hir quhite lyre,
Hir hair is like the goldin wyre:
My hart burnis in ane flame of fyre
I sweir yow be the Rude.
I think scho is sa wonder fair,

94

That in earth scho hes na compair,
War ye weill leirn it at lulfis lair
And syne had hir anis sene:
I wait be cokis passioun,
Ye wald mak supplicatioun,
And spend on hir ane millioun
Hir lufe for till obteine.

SOLACE: Quhat say ye sir ar ye content,
That scho cum heir incontinent:
Quhat vails your kingdome and your rent,
And all your great treasure:
Without ye haif ane mirrie lyfe,
And cast asyde all sturt and stryfe —
And sa lang as ye want ane wyfe,
Fall to and tak your pleasure.

REX: Gif that be trew quhilk ye me tell,
I will not langer tarie:
Bot will gang preif that play my sell,
Howbeit the warld me warie.
Als fast as ye may carie,
Speid with all diligence:
Bring Sensualitie,
Fra-hand to my presence.
Forsuth I wait not how it stands,
Bot sen I hard of your tythands,
My bodie trimblis feit and hands
And quhiles is hait as fyre:
I trow Cupido with his dart,
Hes woundit me out — throw the hart
My spreit will fra my bodie part,
Get I nocht my desyre.
Pas on away with diligence,
And bring hir heir to my presence:
Spair nocht for trauell nor expence·
I cair not for na cost:
Pason your way schone Wantonnes,
And tak with yow Sandie solace,
And bring that Ladie to this place,
Or els I am bot lost.
Commend me to that sweitest thing,
And present hir with this same Ring·
And say I ly in languisching,
Except scho mak remeid:
With siching sair I am bot schent,
Without scho cum incontinent,
My heauie lang our to relent,
And saif me now fra deid.

WANTONNES: Or ye tuik skaith be Gods goun,
    I leuer thair war not up nor doun
    Ane tume cunt into this toun,
    Nor twentie myle about.
    Doubt ye nocht Sir, bot wee will get hir,
    Wee sall be feirie for till fetch hir,
    Bot faith wee wald speid all the better,
    Till gar our pursses rout –

SOLACE: Sir let na sorrow in yow sink,
    Bot gif us Ducats for till drink:
    And wee sall never sleip ane wink
    Till it be back or eadge:
    Ye ken weill Sir wee haue no cunye,

REX: Solace, sure that sall be no sunyie,
    Beir ye that bag upon your lunyie,
    Now sirs win weill your wage;
    I pray yow speid yow sone againe

WANTONNES: Ye of this sang sir wee ar faine,
    Wee sall nether spair wind nor raine
    Till our days wark be done:
    Fairweill for wee ar at the flicht,
    Placebo rewll our Roy at richt:
    We sall be heir man or midnicht,
    Thocht wee marche with the Mone.
    Pastyme with pleasance & greit prosperitie
    Be to yow Soveraine Sensualitie,

SENSUALITIE: Sirs ye ar welcum quhair go ye? eist or west?

WANTONNES: In faith I trow we be at the farrest.

SENSUALITIE: Quhat Is your name I pray you Sir declair?

WANTONNES: Marie Wantonnes the Kings secretair,

SENSUALITIE: Quhat King is that quhilk hes sa gay a boy?

WANTONNES: Humanitie that richt redoutit Roy,
    Quhilk dois commend him to yow hartfullie
    And sends yow heir ane ring with ane Rubie
    In takin that abuife all creatour
    He hes chosen yow to be his Paramonr:
    He bade me say that he will be bot deid,
    Without that ye mak haistelle remeid.

SENSUALITIE: How can I help him althocht he suld for fair –
    Ye ken richt weill I am na Medcinair.

SOLACE: Yes lustie ladie thocht he war never sa seik,

    I wait ye beare his health into your breik:
    Ane kis of your sweit mow in ane morning,
    Till his seiknes micht be greit comforting,
    And als he maks yow supplicatioun,
    This nicht to mak with him collatioun.

SENSUALITIE: I thank his grace of his benevolence,
    Gude sirs I sall be reddie evin fra hand:
    In me thair all be fund a negligence,
    Baith nicht & day quhen his grace will demand,
    Pas ye befoir and say I am cummand,
    And thinks richt lang to haif of him ane sicht:
    And I to Venus do mak ane faithfull band,
    That i his arms I think to ly all nicht.

WANTONNES: That sall be done, bot yit or I hame pas,
    Heir I protest for Hamelynes your las.

SENSUALITIE: Scho salbe at command sir quhen ye will
    I traist scho sall find yow flinging your fill.

WANTONNES: Now hay for joy and mirth I dance,
    Tak thair ane gay gamond of France:
    Am I nocht worthie till avance?
    That am sa gude a page:
    And that sa spedelie can rin,
    To tyst my maister unto sin,
    The feind a penny he will win
    Of this his mariage.
    I rew richt sair be sanct Michell,
    Nor I had pearst hir my awin sell:
    For quhy yon King be Bryds bell
    Kennis na mair of ane cunt:
    Nor dois the noueis of ane freir:
    It war bot almis to pull my eir,
    That wald not preif yon gallant geir:
    Fy that I am sa blunt.
    I think this day to win grelt thank,
    Hay, as ane brydlit cat I brank:
    Alace I haue wreistit my schank,
    Yit gangis be sanct Michaell.
    Quhilk of my leggis Sirs as ye trow,
    Was it that I did hurtevin now?
    Bot quhairto sould I speir at yow
    I think thay baith ar hiall.
    Gude morrow Maister be the Mes,

REX: Weicum my menyeon Wantonnes,
    How hes thow sped in thy trauell?

WANTONNES: Rycht weill be him that herry it hell:
    Your erand is weill done.

REX: Then Wantonnes how weill is mee,
    Thow hes deseruit baith meit and fie,
    Be him that maid the Mone:
    Thair is anething that I wald speir,
    Quhat sall I do quhen scho cums heir?
    For I knaw nocht the craft perqueir
    Of luifers gyn:
    Thairfoir at lenth ye mon me leir
    How to begin.

WANTONNES: To kis hir & clap hir sir be not affeard,
    Sho will not schrink thocht ye kis hir ane span wthin the baird
    Gif ye think that sho thinks shame then hyd ye bairnseine
    With hir taill, & tent hir weil, ye wait quhat I meine:
    Will ye leif me Sir first for to go to,
    And I sall leirne yow all kewis how to do.

REX: God forbid Wantonnes that I gif the leife,
    Thou art ouer perillous ane page sic practiks to preife.

WANTONNES: Now Sir preife as ye pleis, I se hir cumand,
    Use your self grauelie, wee sall by yow stand.

SENSUALITIE: O Queene Venus unto thy Celsitude,
    I gif gloir, honour, laud and reuerence:
    Quha grantit me sic perfite pulchritude,
    That Princes of my persone haue pleasance.
    I mak ane vow with humbill obseruance,
    Richt reuerentlie thy Tempill to visie,
    With sacrifice unto thy Dyosie.
    Till everie stait I am so greabill,
    That few or nane refuses me at all:
    Paipis, Patriarks or Prelats venerabill,
    Common pepill and Princes temporall,
    Ar subiect all to me Dame Sensuall.
    Sa sall it be ay quhill the warld indures
    And speciallie quhair youthage hes the cures.
    Quha knawis the contrair
    I traist few in this companie,
    Wald thay declair the veritie,
    How thay use Sensualitie:
    Bot with me maks repair.
    And now my way I man auance,
    Unto ane Prince of great puissance,
    Quhom young men hes in gouernance
    Rolland into bis rage:
    I am richt glaid I yow assure,

That potent Prince to get in cure:
Quhilk is of lustines the luir,
And greitest of curage.
O potent Prince of pulchritude preclair,
God Cupido preserue your celsitude:
And Dame Venus mot keip your court from cair
As I wald sho suld keip my awin hart-blud:

REX: Welcum to me peirles in pulchritude,
Welcum to me thow sweiter nor the Lamber,
Quhilk hes maid me of all dolour denude,
Solace, convoy this Ladie to my chamber.

SENSUALITIE: I gang this gait with richt gude will,
Sir Wantonnes tarie ye stil:
And Hamelines the cap yeis fill
And beir him cumpanie.
That sall I do withoutin dout,
And he and I sall play cap'out,

WANTONNES: Now Ladie len me that batye tout
Fill in for I am dry.
Your dame be this trewlie,
Hes gotten upon the gumis
Quhat rak thocht ye and I
Go lunne our iusting Lumis,

HAMELINES: Content I am with gude will,
Quhen euer ye ar reddie:
Your pleasure to fulfill,

WANTONNES: Now weill said be our Ladie,
He bair my Maister cumpanie,
Till that I may indure:
Gif ye be quisland wantounlie,
We sall fling on the flure.

GUDE COUNSALL: Immortall God maist of magnificence,
Quhais Maiestie na Clark can comprehend:
Must saue yow all that giuis sic audience,
And grant yow grace him never till offend,
Quhilk on the Croce did willinglie ascend,
And sched his pretious blude on everie side:
Quhais pitious passioun from danger yow defend,
And be your gratious governour and gyde.
Now my gude freinds considder I yow beseik
The caus maist principall of my cumming,
Princis or Potestatis ar nocht worth ane leik,
Be thay not gydit be my gude gouerning:
Thair was never Empriour, Conquerour nor King

Without my wisdome that micht thair wil avance,
My name is Gude Counsall without feinyeing,
Lords for lack of my lair ar brocht to mischance.
Finallie for conclusioun,
Quha halds me at delusioun:
Sall be brocht to confusioun:
And this I understand,
For I haue maid my residence,
With hie Princes of greit puissance,
In Ingland, Italie and France,
And monie uther Land.
Bot out of Scotland wa alace,
I haif bene fleimit lang tyme space,
That garris our gyders all want grace
And die befoir thair day:
Becaus thay lychtlyit gude counsall,
Fortune turnit on thame hir sall,
Quhilk brocht this Realme to meikill baill,
Quha can the contrair say?
My Lords I came nocht heir to lie:
Waes me for King Humanitie,
Owreset with Sensualitie,
In tr'entrie of his ring:
Throw vicious counsell insolent,
Sa thay may get riches or rent,
To his weilfair thay tak na tent,
Nor quhat sai be th'ending.
Yit in this Realme I wald mak sum repair,
Gif I beleifit my name suld nocht forfair,
For wald this King be gydit yit with ressoun,
And on misdoars mak punitioun:
Howbeit I haif lang tyme bene exyllit,
I traist in God my name sall yit be styllit.
Sa till I se God send mair of his grace,
I purpois tilrepois me in this place.

FLATTERIE: Mak roume sirs hoaw, that I may rin,
Lo se quhair I am new cum,
Legaryit all with sindrie hewis:
Let be your din till I begin,
And I sall schaw yow of my newis.
Throucout all Christindome I haue past,
And am cum heir now at the last,
Tostit on sea ay sen Yuill day:
That wee war faine to hew our Mast,
Nocht half an e myle beyond the May.
Bot now amang yow I will remaine,
I purpois never to sall againe:

To put my lyfe in chance of watter:
Was never sene sic wind and raine,
Nor of Schipmen sic clitter clatter.
Sum bade haill and sum bade standby,
On steirburd hoaw aluiff fy fy:
Quhill all the raipis beguith to rattil:
Was never Roysa fleyd as I,
Quhen all the salls playd brittill brattill.
To se the waws it was ane wonder,
And wind that raif the salls in sunder,
Bot I lay braikand like ane Brok:
And shot sa fast aboue and under,
The Deuill durst not cum neir my dok.
Now am I scapit fra that effray,
Quhat say ye sirs am I nocht gay?
Se ye not Flatterie your awin fuill?
That yeid to mak this new array,
Was I not heir with yow at Ɏuill?
Ɏes be my faith I think on weill.
Quhair ar my fallows that wald nocht fail?
We suld haue cum heir for ane cast.
Hoaw Falset hoaw.—

FALSET: — Wa sair the Deuill
Quha is that that cryis for mesa fast

FLATTERIE: Quhy Falset brother knawis thou not me?
Am I nocht thy brother Flattrie?

FALSET: Now welcome be the Trinitie
This meitting cums for gude
Now let me bresse the my armis,
Quhen freinds meits harts warmis:
Quod lok that frelie fud:
How happinit yow into this place?

FLATTERIE: Now be my saul evin on a cace.
I come in sleipand at the port,
Or ever I wist amang this sort,
Quhair is Dissait that limmer loun?

FALSET: I left him drinkand in the toun,
He will be heir incontinent.

FLATTERIE: Now be the haly Sacrament,
Thay tydingis comforts all my hart:
I wait Dissait will tak my part.
He is richt craftie as ye ken,
And counsallour to the Merchand-men:
Let us ly doun heir baith and spy,
Gif wee persaue him cummand by.

DISSAIT: Stand by the gait that I maysteir,
 Aisay Koks bons, how cam I heir?
 can not mis to tak sum feir,
 Into sa greit ane thrang:
 Marie heir ane cumlie congregatioun,
 Quhat ar ye sirs all of ane natioun?
 Maisters I speik be protestatioun,
 In dreid ye tak me wrang.
 Ken ye not sirs quhat is my name?
 Gude faith I dar not schawit for schame:
 Sen I was clekit of my Dame,
 Yit was I never leill:
 For Katie unsell was my mother,
 And common theif my father-brother:
 Offic freindship I had ane fither,
 Howbelt I can not steill.
 Bot yit I will borrow and len,
 As be my deathlng ye may ken;
 That I am cum of nobill men,
 And als I will debait,
 That querrell with my felt and hands:
 And I dwell amang the merchands,
 My name gifonie man demands,
 Thay call me Dissait –
 Bon-iour brother with all my hart,
 Heir I am cum to tak your part,
 Balth Into gude and euill:
 I met Gude counsall be the way,
 Quha pat me in ane felloun fray,
 I gif him to the Deuill.

FALSET: How chaipit ye I pray yow tell?

DISSAIT: I slipit into ane bordell:
 And hid me in ane bawburds bed:
 Bot suddenlie hir schankis I sched
 With hoch hurland amang hir howls
 God wait gif wee maid monie mowis:
 How came ye heir I pray yow tell me?

FALSET: Marie to seik King Humanitie.

DISSAIT: Now be the gude Ladie that me bair,
 That samin hors is my awin Mair:
 Now with our purpois let us mell,
 Quhat is your counsall I pray yow tell?
 Sen we thrie seiks yon nobill King,
 Let us deuyse sum subtil! thing:
 And als I pray yow as my brother,

That we ilk ane be trew to uther.
I mak ane vow with all my hart,
In gude and euill to tak your part,
I pray to God nor I be hangit,
Bot I sall die or ye be wrangit.

FALSET: Quhat is thy counsall that wee do?
Marie sirs this is my counsall lo,
Till tak our tyme quhili wee may get it,
For now thait is na man to let it:
Fra tyme the King begin to steir him,
Marie gude counsall I dreid cum neir him,
And be wee knaw in with Correctioun.
It will be our confusioun:
Thairfoir my deir brother deuyse
To find sum toy of the new gyse.

FLATTERIE: Marie I sall finde ane thousand wyles,
Wee man turne our claithis & change our stiles:
And diasagyse us that na man ken us,
Hes na man Clarkis cleathing to len us:
And let us keip graue countenance,
As wee war new cum out of France.

DISSAIT: Now be my saull that is weill deuysit,
Ye sall se me sone disagysit,

FALSET: And sa sall I man be the Rude,
Now sum gude fallow len me ane hude.

DISSAIT: Now am I buskit and quha can spy,
The Deuill stik me gif this be I:
If this be I or not, I can not weill say,
Or hes the Feind or Fatie-folk borne me away,

FALSET: And gif my hair war up in ane how,
The feind ane man wald ken me I trow:
Quhat sayis thou of my gay garmoun-

DISSAIT: I say thou luiks euin like ane loun:
Now brother Flatterie quhat do ye,
Quhat kynde of man schaip ye to be?

FLATTERIE: Now be my faith my brother deir,
I will gang counterfit the Freir,

DISSAIT: A Freir, quhairto ye can nor preiche.

FLATTERIE: Quhat rak man I can richt weill fleich?
Perchance Ile cum that honour,
To be the Kings confessour.
Pure Freirs ar free at any fealt,

And marchellit ay amang the best.
Als God to hes lent them sic graces,
That Bischops puts them in thair places:
Out-throw thair Dioceis to preiche,
Bot ferlie nocht howbelt thay fleich:
For schaw thay all the veritle,
Thaill want the Bischops charitie.
And thocht the corne war never sa skant,
The gudewyfis will not let Freirs want:
For quhy thay ar thair confessours,
Thair heauinlie prudent counsalours.
Thairfoir the wyfis plainlie taks thair parts,
And shawis the secreits of thair harts,
To Freirs with better will I trow,
Nor thay do to thair bed-fallow.
Dissait, And I reft anis ane Freirs coull,
Bvtuix Sanct-Iohnestoun and Kinnoull:
I sall gang fetch it, gif ye will tarie.

FLATTERIE: Now play me that of companarie.
Ye faw him nocht this hundreth yeir,
That better can counterfeit the Freir.

DISSAIT: Heir is the gaining all and sum,
That is ane koull of Tullilum.

FLATTERIE: Quha hes ane portouns for to len me?
The feind ane saull I trow will ken me.

FALSET: Now gang thy way quhalr euer thow will,
Thow may be fallow to freir Gill:
Bot with Correctioun gif wee be kend,
I dreid wee mak ane schamefull end.

FLATTERIE: For that mater I dreid nathing,
Freiris ar exemptit fra the King:
And Freiris will reddie entries get,
Quhen Lords ar haldin at the yet.

FALSET: Wee man do mair yit be Sanct Iames,
For wee mon all thrie change our names
Hayif me, and Isali baptize thee:

DISSAIT: Be God and thair – about may it be.
How will thou call me I pray the tell?

FALSET: I wait not how to call my sell.

DISLAIT: Bot yit anis name the bairns name,

FALSET: Discretioun, Discretioun in Gods name.

DISLAIT: I neid nocht now to cair for thrift,
  Bot quhat salbe my God bairne gift?

FALSET: I gif yow all the Deuilis of hell,

DISSAIT: Na brother hauld that to thy sel.
  Now sit doun let me baptize the
  I wait not quhat thy name sould be:

FALSET: Bot yit anis name the bairns name.
  Dissait Sapience in ane warlds-schame.

FLATTERIE: Brother Dissait cum baptize me,

DISSAIT: Then sit doun lawlie on thy kne.

FLATTERIE: Now brother name the bairns name,

DISSAIT: Devotioun the Deuillis name,

FLATTERIE: The deuill resaue the lurdoun loun,
  Thow hes weat all my new schawin croun.

DISSAIT: Devotioun, Sapience and discretioun,
  Wee thre may rewll this Regioun.
  Wee sall find monie craftie things,
  For to begyll are hundreth Kingis.
  For thow can richt weil crak and clatter,
  And I sall feinye, and thow sall flatter.

FLATTERIE: Bot I wald haue or wee depairtit,
  Ane drink to mak us better hartit.

Now the King sall cum fra his chamber.

DISSAIT: Weill said be him that herryit hell,
  I was euin thinkand that my sell.
  Now till wee get the Kings presence,
  Wee will sit down and keip silence:
  Ise ane yeoman quhat ever be,
  Ile wod my lyfe yon same is he.
  Feir nocht brother, bot hauld yow still,
  Till wee haue hard quhat is his will.

REX: Now quhair is Placebo and Solace?
  Quhair is my minyeoun Wantonnes?
  Wantonnes hoaw, cum to me sone,

WANTONNES: Quhy cryit ye sir till I had done?

REX: Quhat was ye doand tell me that?

WANTONNES: Mary leirand how my father me gat.
  I wait nocht how it stands but doubt.
  Me think the warld rinnis round about.

REX: And sa think I man be my thrift
    I se fyteine Mones in the lift.

HAMELIN: Gat ye nocht that quhilk ye desyrit?
    Sir I beleif that ye ar tyrit.

DANGER: Bot as for Placebo and Solace
    I held them baith in mirrines,

SOLACE: Now schaw me sir I yow exhort,
    How ar ye of your luif content
    Think ye not this ane mirrie sport:

REX: Yea that I do in verament.
    Quhat bairnis ar yon upon the bent,
    I did nocht se them all this day.

WANTONNES: Thay will be heir incontinent,
    Stand still and heir quhat thay will say.

Now the Vycis cums and maks salutatioun, saying.

DISSAIT: Laud honor, gloir, triumph & victory
    Be to your maist excellent Maiestie.

REX: Ye ar welcum gude freinds be the Rude,
    Appeirandlie ye seime sum men of gude,
    Quhat ar your names tell me without delay,

DISSAIT: Discretioun Sir, is my name perfay.

REX: Quhat is your name sit with the clipit croun

FLATTERIE: But dout my name is callit Devotioun.

REX: Welcum Devotioun be Sanct Iame:
    Now siray tell quhat is your name?

FALSET: Marie sir thay call me, quhat call thay me?

REX: Can ye nocht tell quhat is your name?

FALSET: I kend it quhen I cam fra hame.

REX: Quhat gars ye can nocht schawit now?

FALSET: Marie thay call me thin-drink I trow?

REX: Thin-drink quhat lynde of name is that?

DISSAIT: Sapiens thou semis to beir ane plat,
    Me think thow schawis the not weill wittit;

FALSET: Sypeins, sir sypeins, marie now ye hit it.

FLATTERIE: Sir gif ye pleis to let him say,
    His name is SAPIENTIA.

FALSET: That same is it be Sanct Michell.

REX: Quhy could thou not tell it thy sell?

FALSET: I pray your grace appardoun me,
　　And I sall schaw the veritie:
　　I am sa full of Sapience,
　　That sumtyme I will tak ane trance.
　　My spreit wes reft fra my bodie,
　　Now heich aboue the Trinitie.

REX: Sapience suld be ane man of gude:

FALSET: Sir ye may ken that be my hude.

REX: Now haue I Sapience and Discretioun,
　　How can I faill to rewll this Regioun?
　　And Devotioun to be my confessour,
　　Thir thrie came in ane happie hour,
　　Heir I mak the my secretar,
　　And thow salbe my thesaurar:
　　And thow salbe my counsallour,
　　In spriruall things and confessour

FLATTERIE: I sweir to yow sir be sanct An,
　　Ye met never with ane wyser man,
　　For monie a craft sir do I can,
　　War thay weill knawin.
　　Sir I haue na feill of flattrie,
　　Bot fosterit with Philsophie,
　　Ane strange man in Astronomie,
　　Quhilk salbe schawin.

FALSET: And I haue greit intelligence
　　In quelling of the quintessence:
　　Bot to preif my experience,
　　Sir len me fourtie crownes:
　　To mak multiplicatioun,
　　And tak my obligatioun,
　　Gif wee mak fals narratioun,
　　Hauld us for verie lownes.

DISSAIT: Sir I ken be your Physnomie,
　　Ye sall conqueis, or els I lie,
　　Danskin, Denmark, and Almane,
　　Spittelfeild and the Realme of Spane.
　　Ye sall haue at your governance.
　　Ranfrow and all the Realme of France.
　　Yea Rugland and the toun of Rome,
　　Castorphine and al christindome.
　　Quhairto sir be the Trinitie,
　　A per se!

FLATTERIE: Sir quhen I dwelt in Italie,
    I leirit the craft of Palmistrie,
    Schaw me the lufe Sir, of your hand,
    And I sall gar yow understand,
    Gif your grace be infortunat,
    Or gif ye be predestinat.
    I see ye will haue fyfteine Queenes
    And fyfteine scoir of Concubeines:
    The Virgin Marie saife your grace,
    Saw ever man sa quhyte ane face:
    Sa greit ane arme, sa fair ane hand,
    Thairs nocht sic ane leg in al this land.
    War ye in armis I think na wonder,
    Howbeit ye dang doun fyfteine hunder.

DISSAIT: Now be my saull thats trew thow sayis
    Wes never man set sa weill his clais:
    Thair is na man in Christintie,
    Sa meit to be ane King as ye,

FALSET: Sir thank the haly Trinitie:
    That send us to your cumpanie:
    For God nor I gaip in ane gallows,
    Gif ever ye fand thrie better fallows.

REX: Ye ar richt welcum be the Rude,
    Ye seime to be thrie men of gude.

Heir sall Gude-Counsell schaw himself in the feild

    Bot quha is yon that stands sa still?
    Ga spy and speir quhat is his will.
    And gif he yearnis my presence,
    Bring him to mee with Diligence.

DISSAIT: That sall wee do be Gods breid:
    We's bring him eather quick or deid.

REX: I will sit still heir and repois,
    Speid yow agane to me my lois,

FALSET: Ye hardlie Sir, keip yow in clois
    And quyet till wee cum againe:
    Brother I trow be coks toes,
    Yon bairdit bogill cums fra ane traine.

DISSAIT: Gif he dois sa he salbe slaine,
    I doubt him nocht, nor yit ane uther:
    Trowit I that he come for ane traine,
    Of my freindis I sould rais ane futher.

FLATTERIE: I doubt full sair be God him sell,

        That yon auld churle be Gude-counsell:
        Get he anis to the Kings presence,
        We thrie will get na audience.

DISSAIT: That matter I sall tak on hand,
        And say it is the Kings command,
        That he a none devoyd this place,
        And cum nocht neir the Kings grace:
        And that under the paine of tressoun:

FLATTERIE: Brother I hauld your counsell ressoun.
        Now let us heir quhat he will say,
        Auld lyart beard, gude day, gude day.

GUDE-COUNSELL: Gude day againe sirs be the rude
        The Lord mot mak yow men of gude.

DISSAIT: Pray nocht for us to Lord nor Ladie,
        For we ar men of gude alreadie,
        Sir schaw to us quhat is your name?

GUDE-COUNSALL: Gude-counsell thay call me at hame,

FALSET: Quhat says thow carle, ar thow Gude-counsell?
        Swyith pak the sone unhappie unsell.
        Gif ever thou cum this gait againe,
        I vow to God thou sall be slaine.

GUDE-COUNSELL: I pray yow sirs, gif me licence,
        To cum anis to the Kings presence:
        To speik bot twa words to his grace,

FLATTERIE: Swyith horsune carle, devoyd this place.

GUDE-COUNSELL: Brother I ken yow weill aneuch,
        Howbeit ye mak it never sa teuch:
        Flattrie, Dissait and Fals-report,
        That will not suffer to resort:
        Gude-Counsall to the Kings presence.

DISSAIT: Suyith hursun carle gang pak thee hence,
        Gif ever thou cum this gait agane,
        I vow to God thousall be slaine.

Heir sall thay hurle away Gude-Counsell.

        Sen at this tyme I can get na presence,
        Is na remeid bot tak in patience.
        Howbeit Gude-counsall haistelie be nocht hard
        With young Princes yit sould thay noch be skard.
        Bot quhen youthheid hes blawin his wanton blast,
        Then fall Gude-counsall rewll him at the last.

Now the Vycis gangs to ane counsall.

FLATTERIE: Now quhill Gude-Counsall is absent,
    Brother wee mon be diligent:
    And mak betwix us sikker bands,
    Quhen vacadns fallis in onie Lands.
    That everie man help weill his fallow,

DISSAIT: I had deir brother be Alhallow.
    Sa ye fische nocht within our bounds,

FLATTERIE: That sall I noch be Gods wounds –
    Bot I sall plainlie tak your partis,

FALSET: Sa sall wee thyne with all our hartis.
    Bot haist us quhill the King is young,
    Let everie man keip weill ane toung.
    And in ilk quarter haue ane spy,
    Us till adverteis haistelly,
    Quhen ony casualities,
    Sall happin into our countries,
    And let us mak provisioun,
    Or he cum to discretioun,
    Na mair he waits now nor ane sant,
    Quhat thing it is to haif or want,
    Or he cum till his perfyte age,
    We sall be sikker of our wage:
    And then let everie carle craif uther.

DISSAIT: Yat mouth spick mair my awin deir brother.
    For God nor I rax in ane raip,
    Thow may gif counsall to the Paip.

Now thay returne to the King.

REX: Quhat gart you bid sa lang fra my presence?
    I think it lang since ye depairtit thence.
    Quhat man was yon with an greit bostous beird
    Me thocht he maid yow all thrie very feard.

DISSAIT: It was ane laidlie lurdan loun,
    Cumde to break buithis into this toun:
    Wee haue gat bind him with ane poill,
    And send him to the theisis hoill:

REX: Let him sit thair with ane mischance, .
    And let us go to our pastance.

WANTONNES: Better go reuell at the rackat,
    Or ellis go to the hurlie hackat,
    Or then to schaw our curtlie corsses,
    Ga se quha best can rin thair horsses.

SOLACE: Na soveraine or wee farther gang
    Gar Sensualitie sing ane sang.

**Heir sall the Ladies sing ane sang – the King sall ly doun amang the Ladies
and then Veritie sall enter.**

VERITIE: *Diligite Iustitiam qui iudicatis terram.*
    Luif Iustice ye quha hes ane Iudges cure,
    In earth and dried the awfull Iudgement,
    Of him that sall cum iudge baith rich and pure,
    Rycht terribilly with bludy wounds rent.
    That dreidfull day into your harts imprent:
    Beleuand weill how and quhat maner ye
    Use Iustice heir til uthers, thair at lenth
    That day but doubt sa sallye judgit be.
    Wo than and duill be to yow Princes all,
    Suffer and the pure anes for till be opprest:
    In everlasting burn and fyre ye sall
    With Lucifer richt dulfullie be drest.
    Thairfoir in tyme for till eschaip that nest,
    Feir God, do law and Iustice equally,
    Till everie man: se that na puir opprest
    Up to the hevin on yow ane vengence cry.
    Be iust iudges without fauour or fead,
    And hauld the Ballance euin till everie wicht:
    Let not the fault be left into the head,
    Then sall the members reulit be at richt.
    For quhy subiects do follow day and nicht
    Thair governours in vertew and in vyce.
    Ye ar the lamps that sould schaw them the licht
    Lo leid them on this sliddrie rone of yce.
    Mobile mutatur semper cum principe vulgus.

    And gif ye wald your subiectis war weill geuin,
    Then verteouslie begin the dance your sell:
    Going befoir then they anone I wein,
    Sall follow yow, eyther till heuin or hell:
    Kings sould of gude exempils be the well,
    Bot gif that your strands be intoxicate,
    In steid of wyne thay drink the poyson fell:
    Thus pepill follows ay thair principate.
    Sic luceat lux vestra coram hominibus, ut videant opera vestra bona.

    And speciallyye Princes of the Preists,
    That of peopill hes spiritual cuir,
    Daylyye sould revolue into your breistis,
    How that thir haly words ar still maist sure
    In verteous lyfe gif that ye do indure
    The pepill wil tak mair tent to your deids

Then to your words: and als baith rich and puir
Will follow yow baith in your warks and words.

Heir sall Flatterie spy Veritie with ane dum countenance.

Gif men of me wald haue intelligence,
Or knaw my name, thay call me VERITIE.
Of Christis law I haue experience,
And hes over salllit many stormie sey.
Now am I seikand King Humanitie,
For of his grace I haue gude esperance,
Fra tyme that he acquaintit be with mee,
His honour and heich gloir I sall avance.

Heir sall Veritie pas to hir sait.

DISSAIT: Gude day father, quhair haue ye bene?
Dectair till us of your nouets.
Flattrie Thair is now lichtit on the grene.
Dame Veritie, be Buiks and bels.
Bot cum scho to the Kings presence
Thair is na buit for us to byde.
Thairfoir I red us all go hence.

FALSET: That will we nocht yit be Sanct Bryde
Bot wee sall ather gang or ryde,
To Lords of Spritualitie,
And gar them trow yon bag of pryde,
Hes spokin manifest heresie.

Heir thay cum to the Spiritualitie.

FLATTERIE: O reverent fatheris of the Sprituall stait,
Wee counsall yow be wyse and vigilant:
Dame Veritie hes lychtit now of lait,
And in hir hand beirand the Newtestament·
Be scho ressauit but doubt wee ar bot schent,
Let hir nocht ludge thairfoir into this Land,
And this wee reid yow do incontinent,
Now quhill the King is with his luif sleipand.

SPRITUALITIE: Wee thank yow freinds of your benevolence,
It sall be done evin as ye haue devysit:
Wee think ye serue ane gudlie recompence,
Defendand us that wee be nocht supprysit.
In this mater wee man be weill aduysit,
Now quhill the King misknawis the veritie,
Be scho ressauit then wee will be deprysit,
Quhat is your counsell brother now let se?

ABBOT: I hauld it best that wee incontinent,
    Gar hauld hir fast into Captivitie:
    Unto the thrid day of the Parlament
    And then accuse hir of hir herisie:
    Or than banische hir out of this cuntrie,
    For with the King gif Veritie be knawin.
    Of our greit gloir wee will degradit be
    And all our secreits to the commouns schawin.

PERSONE: Yese the King is yit effeminate,
    And gydit be Dame Sensualitie,
    Rycht sa with young counsall intoxicate,
    Swa at this tyme ye haif your libertie.
    To tak your tyme I hauld it best for me,
    And go distroy all thir Lutherians:
    In speciall yon ladie Veritie,

SPIRITUALITIE: Sir Persone ye sall be my commissair,
    To put this mater till executioun.
    And ye sir Freir, becaus ye can declair
    The haill processe, pas with him in commissioun,
    Pas all togidder with my braid bennisoun,
    And gifscho speiks against our libertie,
    Then put hir in perpetuall presoun,
    That scho cum nocht to King Humanitie.

Heir sall thay pas to Veritie.

PERSONE: Lustie Ladie we wald faine understand,
    Quhat earand ye haif in this Regioun?
    To preich or teich quha gaif to yow command,
    To counsall Kingis how gat ye commissioun?
    I dreid without ye get ane remissioun,
    And syne renunce your new opiniones
    The sprituall stait sall put yow to perditioun
    And in the fyre will burne yow flesche and bones.

VERITIE: I will recant nathing that I haue schawin,
    I haue said nathing bot the veritie:
    Bot with the King fra tyme that I be knawin
    I dreid ye spaiks of Spritualitie,
    Sall rew that ever I came in this cuntrie
    For gifthe Veritie plainlie war proclamit,
    And speciallie to the Kings Maiestie,
    For your traditions ye wilbe all defamit.

FLATTERIE: Quhat buik is that harlot into thy hand,
    Out walloway, this is the New Test'ment,
    In Englisch toung, and printit in England,
    Herisie, herisie, fire, fire incontinent.

VERITIE: Forsuith my freind ye haue ane wrang judgement,
 For in this Buik thair is na heresie:
 Botour Christs word, baith dulce and redolent,
 Ane springing well of sinceir veritie.

DISSAIT: Cum on your way for all your yealow locks
 Your vantoun words but doubt ye sall repent:
 This nicht ye sall forfair ane pair of stocks,
 And syne the morne be brocht to thoill judgement

VERITIE: For our christs saik I am richt weill content
 To suffer all thing that sall pleis his grace,
 Howbeit ye put ane thousand to torment,
 Ten hundreth thowsand sall rise into thair place.

Veritie sits doun on hir knies and sayis.

 Get up, thow, thow sleipis all too lang, O Lord,
 And mak sum ressonabill reformatioun
 On them that dois tramp doun thy gracious word,
 And hes ane deidlie indignatioun
 At them quha maks maist trew narratioun:
 Suffer me not Lord mair to be molest,
 Gude Lord, I mak the supplicatioun
 With thy unfreinds let me nocht be supprest:
 Now Lords do as ye list,
 I haue na mair to say.

FLATTERIE: Sit doun and tak yow rest,
 All nicht till it be day.

Thay put Veritie in the stocks and returne to Spiritualitie.

DISSAIT: My Lord wee haue with diligence
 Bucklit up weill yon bledrand baird:

SPRITUALITIE: I think ye serue gude recompence,
 Tak thirten crowns for your rewaird.

VERITIE: The Prophesie of the Propheit Esay
 Is practickit alace, on mee this day:
 Quha said the veritie sould be trampit doun
 Amid the streit, and put in Strang presoun.
 His fyue and fyftie chapter quha list luik,
 Sall find thir words writtin in his Bulk.
 Richt sa Sanct Paull wrytis to Timothie,
 That men sall turne thair earis from veritie.
 Bot in my Lord God I haue esperance,
 He will provide for my deliverance.
 Bot ye Princes of Spiritualise,
 Quha sould defend the sinceir veritie,

I dreid the plagues of Johnes Revelatioun
Sall sal upon your generatioun.
I counsail yow this misse t'amend,
Sa that ye may eschaip that fatall end.

CHASTITIE: How lang sall this inconstant warld indure,
That I sould baneist be sa lang alace:
Few creatures or nane takis on me cure,
Quhiik gars me monie nicht ly harbrieles.
Thocht I haue past all yeir fra place to place,
Amang the Temporal and Spirituall staits:
Nor amang Princes I can get na grace,
Bot boustuouslie am halden at the yetis.

DILIGENCE: Ladie I pray yow schaw me your name.
It dois me noy your lamentatioun,

CHASTITIE: My freind thair of I neid not to think shame,
Dame Chastitie baneist from town to town.

DILIGENCE: Then pas to ladies of Religioun,
Quhiik maks thair vow to obserue Chastitie:
Lo quhair thair sits ane Priores of renown,
Amangs the rest of Spritualitie.

CHASTITIE: I grant yon Ladie hes vowit Chastitie,
For hir professioun thairto sould accord:
Scho maid that vow for ane Abesie,
Bot nocht for Christ Jesus our Lord.
Fra tyme that thay get thair vows, I stand for'd,
Thay banische hir out of thair cumpanie,
With Chastitie thay can mak na concord
Bot leids thair lyfis in Sensualitie,
I sall obserue your counsall gif I may,
Cum on and heir quhat yon Ladie will say?

Chastitie passis to the Ladie Priores and sayis.

My prudent lustie Lastie Priores,
Remember how ye did vow Chastitie:
Madame I pray yow of your gentilnes,
That ye wald pleis to haif of me pitie:
And this ane nicht to gif me harberie,
For this I mak yow supplicatioun
Do ye nocht sa Madame I dreid perdie,
It will becaus of depravatioun.

PRIORES: Pas hynd Madame, be Christ ye cum nocht heir,
Ye ar contrair to my cumplexioun:
Gang seik Judging at sum auld Monk or Freir,
Perchance thay will be your protectioun.

Or to Prelats mak your progressioun,
Quhilks ar obleist to yow als weill as I:
Dame Sensuall hes geuin directioun
Yow till exclude out of my cumpany.

CHASTITIE: Gif ye wald wit mair of the veritie,
I sall schaw yow be sure experience,
How that the Lords of Sprituality,
Hes baneist me, alace, fra thair presence.

Chastitie passes to the Lords of Spiritualitie,

My Lords, laud, gloir, triumph and reverence,
Mot be unto your halie Sprituall stait:
I yow beseik of your benevolence,
To harbry mee that am sa desolait,
Lords I haue past throw mony uncouth schyre,
Bot in this Land I can get na ludgeing
Of my name gif ye wald haif knawledging,
Forsuith my Lords thay call me Chastitie,
I yow beseik of your graces bening.
Gif me ludging this nicht for charitie.

SPRITUALITIE: Pas on Madame we knaw yow nocht
Or be him that the warld wrocht,
Your cumming sall be richt deir cot
Gif ye mak langer tarie.

ABBOT: But doubt wee will baith leif and die
With our luif Sensualitie,
Wee will haif na mair deall with the,
Then with the Queene of Farie.

PERSONE: Pas hame amang the Nunnis and dwell,
Quhilks ar of Chastitie the well:
I traist thay will with Buik and bell,
Ressaue yow in thair Closter.

CHASTITIE: Sir, quhen I was the Nunnis amang,
Out of thair dortour thay mee dang,
And wald nocht let me bide sa lang,
To say my Pater noster.
I se na grace thairfoir to get,
I hauld it best or it be lait,
For till go proue the Temporall stait
Gif thay will mee resaif:
Gud-day my Lord Temporalitie,
And yow merchant of gravitie:
Ful faine wald I haue harberie,
To ludge amang the laif.

TEMPORA: Forsuith wee wald be weil content,
    To harbie yow with gude intent,
    War nocht we haif impediment:
    For quhy we twa ar maryit:
    Bot wist our wyfis that ye war heir,
    Thay wald mak all this town on steir:
    Thairfoir we reid yow rin areir,
    In dreid ye be miscaryit.

CHASTITIE: Ye men of craft of greit ingyne,
    Gif me barbrie for Christis pyne:
    And win Gods bennesone and myne,
    And help my hungrie hart:

SOWTAR: Welcum be him that maid the Mone,
    Till dwell with us till it be lune:
    We sall mend baith your hois and schone,
    And plainlie tak your part.

TAYLOUR: Is this fair Ladie Chastitie?
    Now welcum be the Trinitie:
    I think it war ane great pitie
    That thou should ly thairout:
    Your great displeasour I forthink,
    Sit doun Madame and tak ane drink:
    And let na sorrow in yow sink,
    Bot let us play cap'out.

SOWTAR: Fill in and play cap'out,
    For I am wonder dry:
    The Deuill snyp aff thair snout,
    That haits this company.

JENNIE: Hoaw mynnie, mynnie, mynnie.

TAYLOURS WYFE: Quhat wald thow my deir dochter Jennie?
    Jennie my loy, quhair is thy dadie?

JENNIE: Mary drinkand with ane lustie Ladie,
    Ane fair young mayden cled in quhyte,
    Of quhom my dadie taks delyte,
    Scho hes the the fairest forme of face,
    Furnischit with all kynd of grace:
    I traist gif I can reckon richt,
    Scho schaips to ludge with him all nicht.

SOWTARS WYFE: Quhat dols the Sowtar my gudman?

JENNIE: Mary fillis the cap and turnes the can.
    Or he cum hame be God I trow
    He will be drunkin lyke ane sow.

TAYLOURS WYFE: This is ane greit dispyte I think,
　　For to resaue sic ane kow-clink:
　　Quhat is your counsell that wee do?

SOWTARS WYFE: Cummer this is my counsall lo,
　　Ding ye the tane, and I the uther.

TAYLOURS WYFE: I am content be Gods mother.
　　I think for mee thay huirsone smaiks,
　　Thay serue richt weill to get thair paiks.
　　Quhat maister feind neids all this haist,
　　For it is half ane yeir almaist
　　Sen ever that loun laborde my ledder,

SOWTARS WYFE: God nor my trewker mence ane ledder,
　　For it is mair nor fourtie dayis,
　　Sen ever he cleikit up my clayis:
　　And last quhen I gat chalmer glew,
　　That foull Sowter began till spew.
　　And now thay will sit doun and drink,
　　In company with ane kow-clink.
　　Gif thay haif done us this dispyte
　　Let us go ding them till thay dryte.

Heir the wifis sall chase away Chastitie.

TAYLOURS WYFE: Go hence harlot – how durst thow be sa bauld
　　To ludge with our gudemen but our licence:
　　I mak ane vow to him that Iudas sauld,
　　This rock of myne sall be thy recompence.
　　Schaw me thy name dudron with diligence:

CHASTITIE: Marie Chastitie is my name be Sanct Blais.

TAYLOURS WYFE: I pray God nor he work on the vengence.
　　For I luifit never Chastitie all my dayes.

SOWTARS WYFE: Bot my gudeman the treuth I sall the tell,
　　Gars mee keip Chastitie sair agains my will:
　　Becaus that Monstour hes maid sic ane mint
　　With my bedstaf that dastard beirs ane dint.
　　And als I vow cum thow this gait againe,
　　Thy buttoks salbe beltit be Sanct Blaine.

Heir sall thay speik to thair gudemen and ding them.

TAYLOURS WYFE: Fals hurson carle, but dout thou sall forthink,
　　That evar thow eat or drink with yon kow-clink.

SOWTARS WYFE: I mak ane vow to Sanct Crispine,
　　Ise be revengit on that graceles grume:
　　And to begin the play tak thair ane flap.

SOWTAR: The feind relaue the hands that gaif mee that.

SOWTARS WYFE: Quhat now huirsun, begins thow for til ban?
   Tak thair ane uther upon thy peild harne-pan.
   Quhat now cummer, will thow nocht tak my part?

TAYLOURS WYFE: That sal I do cummer with all my hart.

Heir sall thay ding thair gudemen, with silence.

TAYLOUR: Alace gossop, alace how stands with yow,
   Yon cankart carling alace hes brokin my brow.
   Now weils yow Preists, now weils yow all your lifes,
   That ar nocht weddit with sic wickit wyfes.

SOWTAR: Bischops ar blist howbeit that thay be waryit,
   For thay may fuck thair fill and be vnmaryit.
   Gossop alace, that blak band we may wary,
   That ordanit sic puir men as us to mary.
   Quhat may be done bot tak in patience?
   And on all wyfis we'ill cry ane loud vengence.

Heir sall the wyfis stand be the watter syde and say.

SOWTARS WYFE: Sen of our cairls we haue the victorie,
   Quhat is your counsell cummer that be done:

TAYLOURS WYFE: Send for gude wine & hald our selfis merie,
   I hauid this ay best cummer be Sanct Clone.

SOWTARS WYFE: Cummer will ye draw aff my hois & schone,
   To fill the Quart I sall rin to the toun.

TAYLOURS WYFE: That sal I do be him that maid the Mone
   Withall my hart, thairfoir cummer sit doun.
   Kilt up your claithis abone your waist,
   And speid yow hame againe in haist
   And I sall provyde for ane paist,
   Our corsses to comfort.

SOWTARS WYFE: Then help me for to kilt my clais,
   Quhat gif the padoks nip my tais.
   I dreid to droun heir be Sanct Blais,
   Without I get support.

Sho lifts up hir clais aboue hir waist & enters in ye water.

   Cummer I will nocht droun my sell,
   Go east about the nether mill:

TAYLOURS WYFE: I am content be Bryds bell,
   To gang with yow quhair ever ye will.

Heir sall thay depairt and pas to the Palyeoun.

DILIGENCE: **(to Chastitie)**, Madame quhat gars yow gang sa lait?
    Tell me how ye haue done debait,
    With the Temporall and Spirituall sta it?
    Quha did yow maist kyndnes.

CHASTITIE: In faith I fand bot ill and war,
    Thay gart mee stand fra thame askar:
    Evin lyk ane begger at the bar,
    And fleimit mair and lesse.

DILIGENCE: I counsall yow but tarying,
    Gang tell Humanitie the King:
    Perchance hee of his grace bening
    Will mak to yow support:

CHASTITIE: Of your counsell I am content,
    To pas to him in continent,
    And my service till him present,
    In hope of sum comfort.

Heir sall thay pas to the King.

DILIGENCE: Hoaw Solace, gentil Solace declair unto the king
    How thair is heir ane Ladie fair of face:
    That in this cuntrie can get na ludging,
    Bot pitifullie flemit from place to place,
    Without the king of his speciall grace,
    As ane servand hir in his court resaif:
    Brother Solace tell the king all the cace,
    That scho may-be resavit amang the laif.

SOLACE: Soverane get up and se ane hevinlie sicht
    Ane fair Ladie in quhyt abuilyement:
    Scho may be peir unto ane king or knicht,
    Most lyk ane Angell be my judgement.

REX: I sall gang se that sicht incontinent,
    Madame behauld gif ye haue knawledging
    Of yon Ladie, or quhat is hir intent,
    Thairefter wee sall turne but tarying.

SENSUALITIE: Sir let me se quhat yon mater may meine
    Perchance that I may knaw hir be hir face:
    But doubt this is Dame Chastitie I weine,
    Sir I and scho cannot byde in ane place,
    But gif it be the pleasour of your grace,
    That I remaine into your company:
    This woman richt haistelie gar chase,
    That scho na mair be sene in this cuntry.

REX: As ever ye pleis sweit hart sa sall it be,
    Dispone hir as ye think expedient:
    Evin as ye list to let hir liue or die,
    I will refer that thing to your judgement.

SENSUALITIE: I will that scho be flemit incontinent,
    And never to cum againe in this cuntrie:
    And gif scho dois but doubt scho sall repent,
    As als perchance a duilfull deid sall die.
    Pas on sir Sapience and Discretioun,
    And banische hir out of the kings presence.

DISSAIT: That sall we do Madame be gods passioun,
    Wee sall do your command with diligence.
    And at your hand serue gudely recompence,
    Dame Chastitie cum on, be not agast,
    Wee sall rycht sone upon your awin expence,
    Into the stocks your bony fute mak fast,

Heir sall thay harll Chastitie to the stoks and scho sall say.

I pray yow sirs be patient,
For I sall be obedient
Till do quhat ye command,
Sen I se thair is na remeid,
Howbeit it war to suffer deid,
Or flemit furth of the land.
I wyte the Empreour Constantine,
That I am put to sic ruine,
And baneist from the Kirk:
For sen he maid the Paip ane King,
In Rome I could get na ludging;
Bot heidlangs in the mirk.
Bot Ladie Sensualitie,
Sensyne hes gydit this cuntrie,
And monie ef the rest:
And now scho reulis all this land,
And hes decryit at hir command,
That I suld be supprest.
Bot all comes for the best,
Til him that louis the Lord:
Thocht I be now molest,
I traist to be restorde.

Heir sall they put hir in the stocks.

Sister alace, this is ane cairful cace,
That we with Princes souid be sa abhorde:

VERITIE: Be blyth sister, I trust within schort space,

That we sall be richt honorablie restorde:
And with the King we sall be at concorde,
For I heir tell divyne Correctioun
Is new landit thankit be Christ our Lord,
I wait hee will be our protectioun.

Heir sall enter Corrections Varlet.

VARLET: Sirs stand abak and hauld yow coy,
    I am the King Correctiouns boy,
    Cum heir to dres his place:
    Se that ye mak obedience
    Untill his no bill excellence,
    Fra tyme ye se his face.
    For he maks reformatiouns,
    Out-throw all Christin Natiouns,
    Quhair he finds great debaits.
    And sa far as I understand-
    He sall reforme into this Land,
    Evin all the thrie estaits.
    God furth of heavin hes him send,
    To punische all that dois offend
    Against his Maiestie
    As lyks him best to tak vengence,
    Sumtyme with Sword and Pestilence
    With derth and povertie.
    Bot quhen the peopill dois repent,
    And beis to God obedient,
    Then will he gif them grace:
    Bot thay that will nocht be correctit,
    Rychtsudanlie will be deiectit,
    And fleimit from his face.
    Sirs thocht wee speik in general!,
    Let na man into speciall
    Tak our words at the warst:
    Quhat ever wee do quhat ever wee say
    I pray yow tak it all in play,
    And iudg ay to the best.
    For silence I protest
    Baith of Lord, Laird and Ladie:
    Now I will rin but rest,
    And tell that all is ready.

DISSAIT: Brother heir ye yon proclamatioun,
    I dreid full sair of reformatioun,
    Yon message maks me mang it:
    Quhat is your counsell to me tell,
    Remaine wee heir be God him sell
    Wee will be all thrie hang it.

FLATTERIE: Ile gang to Spiritualitie,
    And preich out-throw his dyosie,
    Quhair I will be unknawin.
    Or keip me closse into sum closter,
    With mony piteous Pater noster,
    Till all thir blasts be blawin.

DISSAIT: Ile be weill treitit as ye ken,
    With my maisters the merchand men;
    Quhilk can mak small debait:
    Ye ken richt few of them that thryfes,
    Or can begyll the landwart wyfes,
    But me thairman Dissait.
    Now Falset quhat sall be thy schift?

FALSET: Na cuir thow nocht man for my thrift
    Trows thou that I be daft:
    Na I will leif ane lustie lyfe,
    Withoutin ony sturt and stryfe
    Amang the men of craft.

FLATTERIE: I na mair will remaine besyd yow,
    Bot counsel! yow rycht welll to gyde yow,
    Byd nocht on Correctioun.
    Fair-weil, I will na langer tarie,
    I pray the allien Queene of Farie,
    To be your protectioun.

DISSAIT: Falset I wald wee maid ane band,
    Now quhill the King is yit sleipand,
    Quhat rack to steill his Box?

FALSET: Now weill said be the Sacrament,
    I sall it steill incontinent
    Thocht it had twentie lox.

Heir sall Falset steill the Kings Box with silence.

    Lo heir the Box now let us ga,
    This may suffice for our rewairds:

DISSAIT: Yea that it may man be this day,
    It may weill mak of landwart lairds.
    Now let us cast away our dais.
    In dreid sum follow on the chase.

FALSET: Rycht weill deuysit man be Sanct Blais,
    Wald God wee war out of this place.

DISSAIT: Now sen thair is na man to wrang us
    I pray yow brother with my hart,

Let us ga part this pelf amang us,
Syne haistely we sall depart.

FALSET: Trows thou to get als mekill as I,
That sall thow nocht, I staw the Box:
Thou did nathing bot luikit by.
Ay lurke and lyke ane wylie Fox.

DISSAIT: Thy heid sall beir ane cuppill of knox
Pellour without I get my part:
Swyith huirsun smaik ryfe up the lox,
Or I sall stick the throuch the hart.

Heir sall thay fecht with silence.

FALSET: Alace for ever my eye is out,
Walloway will na man red the men?

DISSAIT: Upon thy craig tak thair ane clout,
To be courtesse I sall the ken.
Pair-weill, for I am at the flicht,
I will nocht byde on ma demands,
And wee twa meit againe this nicht,
Thy feit salbe with fourtie hands.

Heir sall Dissait rin away with the Box throuch the water.

DIVYNE CORRECTIOUN: *Beati qui esuriunt & sitiunt Iustitiam.*
Thir ar the words of the redoutit Roy,
The Prince of peace aboue all Kings King:
Quhilk hes me sent all cuntries to convoye,
And all misdoars dourlie to doun thring.
I will do nocht without the conveining
Ane Parleament of the estaits all,
In thair presence I sall but feinyeing
Iniquitie under my Sword doun thrall.
Thair may no Prince do acts honorabill,
Bot gif his counsall thairto will assist:
How may he knaw the thing maist profitabil,
To follow vertew and vycis to resist:
Without he be instructit and solist:
And quhen the King stands at his counsell sound,
Then welth sall wax and plentie as he list,
And policie sall in his Realme abound.
Gif ony list my name for till inquyre,
I am callit Divine Correctioun.
I fled throch mony uncouth land & schyre,
To the greit profit of ilk Natioun.
Now am I cum into this Regioun,
To teill the ground that hes bene lang unsawin:

To punische tyrants for thair transgressioun,
And to caus leill men liue upon thair awin.
Na Realme nor Land but my support may stand
For I gar Kings liue into Royaltie:
To rich and puir I beir ane equall band,
That thay may liue into thair awin degrie.
Quhair I am nocht is no tranqullitie
Be me tratours and tyrants ar put doun:
Quha thinks na schame of thair iniquitie
Till thay be punisched be mee Correctioun,
Quhat is ane King nocht bot ane officiar,
To caus his Leiges liue in equitie:
And under God to be ane punischer,
Of trespassours against his Maiestie.
Bot quhen the King dois liue in tyrannie,
Breakand Iustice for feare or affectioun:
Then is his Realme in weir and povertie,
With schamefull slauchter but correctioun.
I am ane Iudge richt potent and seveir,
Cum to do Iustice monie thowsand myle:
I am sa constant baith in peice and weir,
Na bud nor fauour may my sicht oversyle.
Thair is thairfoir richt monie in this Ile,
Of my repair but doubt that dois repent:
Bot verteous men I traist sall on me smyle,
And of my cumming sall be richt weill content.

GUDE-COUNSELL: Welcum my Lord welcum ten thousand tyms
Till all faithfull men of this Regioun,
Welcum for till correct all falts and cryms:
Amang this cankerd congregatioun.
Louse Chastitie I mak supplicatioun,
Put till fredome fair Ladie Veritie:
Quha be unfaithfull folk of this Natioun,
Lyis bund full fast into Captivitie.

CORRECTIOUN: I mervel Gude-counsell how that may be,
Ar ye nocht with the King familiar?

GUDE-COUNSELL: That I am nocht my Lord, full wais me,
Bot lyke ane beggeram halden at the bar:
Thay play bo-keik evin as I war ane skar:
Thair came thrie knaues in cleithing counterfeit
And fra the King thay gart me stand affar.
Quhais names war Flattrie, Falset and Dissait.
Bot quhen thay knaues hard tell of your cumming,
Thay staw away ilk ane ane sindrie gait.
And cuist fra them thair counterfit deithing,
For thair leuing full weill thay can debait:

125

The merchandmen thay haif resauit Dissait.
As for Falset, my Lord, full weill I ken,
He will be richt weill treitit air and lait,
Amang the maist part of the crafts men.
Flattrie hes taine the habite of ane Freir
Thinkand to begyll Spiritualitie.

CORRECTIOUN: But dout my freind and I liue half ane yeit
I sall search out that great iniquitie.
Quhair lyis yon Ladyes in Captiuitie?
How now Sisters quha hes yow sa disgysit?

VERITIE: Unfaithfull members of iniquitie,
Dispytfullie, my Lord, hes us supprysit.

CORRECTIOUN: Gang put yon Ladyis to thair libertie
Incontinent and break doun all the stocks:
But doubt thay ar full deir welcum to mee,
Mak diligence, me think ye do bot mocks
Speid hand and spair nocht for to break the locks,
And tenderlie tak them up be the hand
Had I them heir thay knaues suld ken my knocks
That them opprest and baneist aff the land.

Thay tak the Ladyis furth of the stocks, and Veritie sall say.

VERITIE: Wee thank you sir of your benignitie,
Bot I beseik your maiestie Royall:
That ye wald pas to King Humanitie.
And fleime from him yon Ladie Sensuall,
And enter in his service Gude-counsell,
For ye will find him verie counsalabill.

CORRECTIOUN: Cum on Sisters as ye haif said, I sall,
And gar him stand with yow thrie firme and stabill,

Correctioun passis towards the King with Veritie Chastitie and Gude-counsell.

WANTONNES: Solace knawis thou not quhat I se?
Ane knicht or ellis ane king thinks me,
With wantoun wings as he wald fie,
Brother quhat may this meine?
I understand nocht be this day,
Quhidder that he be freind or fay:
Stand still and heare quhat he will say,
Sic ane I haif nocht seine.

SOLACE: Yon is ane stranger I stand forde,
He semes to be ane lustie Lord:
Be his heir-cumming for concorde,
And be kinde till our King:

He sall be welcome to this place,
And treatit with the Kingis grace:
Be it nocht sa, we sall him chace,
And to the diuell him ding.

PLACEBO: I reid us put upon the King;
And walkin him of his sleiping:
Sir rise and se ane uncouth thing.
Get up, ye ly too lang.

SENSUALITIE: Put on your hude Iohne-Fule, ye raif,
How dar ye be so pertsir knaif
To tuich the King? sa Christ me saif,
Fals huirsone thow sall hang.

CORRECTIOUN: Get up sir King, ye haif sleipit aneuch
Into the armis of Ladie Sensual.
Be suit that mair belangis to the pleuch,
As efterward perchance rehears I sall.
Remember how the King Sardanapall,
Amang fair Ladyes tuke his lust sa lang,
Sa that the maist pairt of his Leiges al
Rebeld, and syne him duilfully doun thrang.
Remember how into the tyme of Noy,
For the foull stinck and sin of lechery,
God be my wande did al the warld destroy,
Sodome and Gomore richt sa full rigorously,
For that vyld sin war brunt in maist cruelly.
Thairfoir I the command incontinent,
Banische from the that huir Sensualitie,
Or els but doubt rudlie thow sall repent.

REX: Be quhom haue ye sa greit authoritie?
Quha dois presume for til correct ane King?
Knaw ye nocht me greit King Humanitie?
That in my Regioun Royally dois ring.

CORRECTIOUN: I haue power greit Princes to doun-thring,
That liues contrair the Maiestie Divyne
Against the treuth quhilk plainlie dois maling,
Repent they nocht I put them to ruyne.
I will begin at thee quhilk is the head,
And mak on the first reformatioun,
Thy Leiges than will follow the but pleid,
Swyith harlot hence without dilatioun.

SENSUALITIE: My Lord I mak yow supplicatioun,
Gif melicence to pas againe to Rome:
Amang the Princes of that Natioun,
I lat yow wit my fresche beautie will blume

Adew Sir King I may na langer tary,
I cair nocht that, als gude luife cums as gais,
I recommend yow to the Queene of Farie.
I se ye will be gydit with my fais,
As for this king I cure him nocht twa strais:
War I amang Bischops and Cardinals,
I wald get gould, silver and precious clais,
Na earthlie joy but my presence avails.

Heir sall scho pas to Spiritualitie.

My Lords of the Sprituall stait,
Venus preserue yow air and lait:
For I can mak na mair debait,
I am partit with your king:
And am baneischt this Regioun,
Be counsell of Correctioun:
Be ye nocht my protectioun,
I may seik my ludgeing.

SPIRITUALITIE: Welcum our dayis darling,
Welcum with all our hart:
Wee all but feinyeing,
Sall plainly tak your part.

Heir sall the Bishops, Abbots and Persons kis the Ladies.

CORRECTIOUN: Sen ye ar quyte of Sensualitie,
Resaue into your service Gude-counsall:
And richt sa this fair Ladie Chastitie,
Till ye mary sum Queene of blude-royall.
Observe then Chastitie matrimoniall,
Richt sa resaue Veritie be the hand,
Use thair counsell your fame sall never fall,
With thame thairfoir mak ane perpetuall band.

Heir sall the King resaue Counsell Veritie & Chastitie.

Now sir tak tent quhat I will say,
Observe thir same baith nicht and day,
And let them never part yow fray.
Or els withoutin doubt:
Turne ye to Sensualitie,
To vicious lyfe and rebaldrie,
Out of your Realme richt schamefullie,
Ye sall be ruttit out.
As was Tarquine the Romane King,
Quha was for his vicious living
And for the schamefull ravisching
Of the fair chaist Lucres,

He was digraidit of his croun,
And baneist aff his Regioun:
I maid on him correctioun,
As stories dois expres.

REX: I am content to your counsall t'inclyne
Ye beand of gude conditioun.
At your command sall be all that is myne,
And heir I gif yow full commissioun,
To punische faults and gifremissioun,
To all vertew I salbe consociabill,
With yow I sall confirme ane unioun,
And at your counsall stand ay firme and stabill.

The king imbraces Correction with a humbil countenance –

CORRECTIOUN: I counsall yow incontinent,
To gar proclame ane Parliament,
Of all the thrie estaits.
That thay be heir with diligence,
To mak to yow obedience,
And syne dres all debaits.

REX: That sall be done but mair demand,
Hoaw Diligence cum heir fra hand,
And tak your informatioun:
Gang warne the Spiritualitie,
Rycht sa the Temporalitie,
Be oppin proclamatioun,
In gudlie haist for to compeir
In thair maist honorabill maneir,
To gif us thair counsals:
Quha that beis absent to them schaw,
That thay sall underly the law,
And punischt be that fails.

DILIGENCE: Sir I sall baith in bruch and land,
With diligence do your command,
Upon my awin expens:
Sir I haue servit yow all this yeir,
Bot I gat never ane dinneir
Yit for my recompence.

REX: Pas on and thou salbe regairdit,
And for thy service weill rewairdit,
For quhy with my consent,
Thou sall haue yeirly for thy hyre,
The teind mussellis of the ferrie myre,
Confirmit in Parliament.

DILIGENCE: I will get riches throw that rent,

Ester the day of Dume:
Quhen in the colpots of Tranent,
Butter will grow on brume.
All nicht I had sa meikill drouth,
I micht nocht sleip ane wink
Or I proclame ocht with my mouth,
But doubt I man haif drink.

CORRECTIOUN: Cum heir Placebo and Solace,
With your companyeoun Wantonnes,
I knaw weill your conditioun:
For tysting King Humanitie,
To resaue Sensualitie,
Ye man suffer punitioun.

WANTON: We grant my lord we haue done ill,
Thairfoir wee put us in your will,
Bot wee haife bene abusit:
For in gudefaith Sir wee beleifit.
That lecherie had na man greifit,
Becaus it is sa usit.

PLACEBO: Ye se how Sensualitie,
With Principals of ilk cuntrie,
Bene glaidlie lettin in:
And with our Prelatis mair and les,
Speir at my Ladie Priores,
Giflechery be sin.

SOLACE: Sir wee sall mend our conditioun,
Sa ye giue us remissioun,
Bot giue us liue to sing:
To dance, to play at Chesse and Tabils,
To reid Stories and mirrie fabils,
For pleasure of our King.

CORRECTIOUN: Sa that ye do navther cryme,
Ye sall be pardon it at this tyme,
For quhy – as I suppois
Princes may sumtyme seik solace,
With mirth and lawfull mirrines,
Thair spirits to reioyis.
And richt sa Halking and Hunting,
Ar honest pastimes for ane King,
Into the tyme of peace:
And leirne to rin ane heavie spear –
That he into the tyme of wear,
May follow at the cheace.

REX: Quhair is Sapience and Discretioun?
And quhy cums nocht Devotioun nar?

VERITIE: Sapience sir was ane verie loun,
    And Discretioun was nathing war:
    The suith Sir, gif I wald report,
    Thay did begyle your Excellence:
    And wald not suffer to resort
    Ane of us thrie to your presence.

CHASTITIE: Thay thrie war Flattrie and Dissait,
    And Falset that unhappie loun:
    Against us thrie quhilk maid debait,
    And baneischt us from town to town.
    Thay gart us twa fall into sowne,
    Quhen thay us lockit in the stocks:
    That dastart knaue Discretioun,
    Full thifte ouslie did steill your Box.

REX: The Deuill tak them sen thay ar gane,
    Me thocht them ay thrie verie smaiks,
    I mak ane vow to Sanct Mavane,
    Quhen I them finde thays bear thair paiks,
    I se thay haue playit me the glaiks,
    Gude-counsall now schaw me the best,
    Quhen I fix on yow thrie my staiks,
    How I sall keip my Realme in rest.
    Initium sapientiae est timor Domini.

GUDE-COUNSELL: Sir, gif your hienes yearnis lang to ring,
    First dread your God abuif all uther thing.
    For ye ar bot ane mortall instrument,
    To that great God and King Omnipotent.
    Preordinat be his divine Maiestie,
    To reull his peopill intill unitie,
    The principall point Sir of ane kings office,
    Is for to do to euerilk man justice.
    And for to mix his justice with mercie,
    But rigour, fauour or parcialitie.
    Forsuith it is na littill obseruance,
    Great Regions to haue in gouernance?
    Quha euer taks on him that kinglie cuir,
    To get ane of thirtwa he suld be suir:
    Great paine and labour, and that continuall,
    Or ellis to haue defame perpetuall.
    Quha guydis weill they win immortall fame,
    Quha the contrair, they get perpetuall schame,
    Efter quhais death but dout ane thousand yeir
    Thair life at lenth rehearst sall be perqueir.
    The Chroniklis to knaw Iyow exhort,
    Thair sall ye finde baith gude and euill report:
    For euerie Prince efter his qualitie,

Thocht he be deid, his deids sall neuer die.
Sir gif ye please for to use my counsall,
Your fame and name sall be perpetuall.

Heir sall the messinger Diligence returne and cry *A Hoyyes, A Hoyyes, A Hoyyes*, and say.

At the command of King Humanitie,
I wairne and charge all members of Parliament:
Baith sprituall stait and Temporalitie,
That till his Grace thay be obedient,
And speid them to the Court incontinent,
In gude ordour array it royally,
Quha beis absent or inobedient
The Kings displeasure they sall underly.
And als I mak yow exhortatioun,
Sen ye haifheard the first pairt of our play:
Go tak ane drink, and mak Collatioun,
Ilk man drink till his marrow, I yow pray.
Tarie nocht lang, it is lait in the day,
Let sum drink Ayle and sum drink Claret wine:
Be great Doctors of Physick I heare say,
That michtie drink comforts the dull ingine.
And ye Ladies that list to pisch,
Lift up your taill, plat in ane disch:
And gif that your mawkine cryis quhisch,
Stop in ane wusp of stray.
Let nocht your bladder burst I pray yow,
For that war euin aneuch to slay yow:
For yit thair is to cum, I say yow,
The best pairt of our Play.

The end of the first part of the Satyre

Now sall the pepill mak Collatioun, then beginnis the Interlude, the Kings, Bischops and principall players being out of their seats.

PAUPER, THE PURE MAN: Of your almis gude folks for Gods luife of heavin,
    For I haue motherles bairns either sax or seavin:
    Gif ye'ill gif me na gude for the luife of Iesus,
    Wische me the richt way till Sanct-Androes.

DILIGENCE: Quhair haue wee gottin this gudly companyeoun?
    Swyith out of the feild fals raggit loun.
    God wait gif heir be ane weill keipit place,
    Quhen sic ane vilde begger Carle may get entres.
    Fy on yow officiars that mends nocht thir failyies,
    I gif yow all till the deuill baith Provost and Bailyies
    Without ye cum and chase this Carle away
    The Deuill a word ye'is get mair of our play.
    Fals huirsun raggit Carle, quhat Deuil is that thou rugs

PAUPER: Quha Devil maid the ane gentill man that wald cut not thy lugs?

DILIGENCE: Quhat now? me thinks the carle begins to crack,
    Swyith carle away or be this day Ise break thy back.

Heir sall the Carle clim up and sit in the Kings tchyre.

    Cum doun, or be Gods croun fals loun I sall slay the.

PAUPER: Now sweir be thy brunt schinis the Deuill ding them fra the.
    Quhatsay ye till thir court dastards be thay get hail clais
    Sa sune as thay leir to sweir and trip on thair tais.

DILIGENCE: Me thocht the carle callit me knaue evin in my face
    Be Sanct Fillane thou salbe slane, bot gif thou ask grace:
    Loup doun or be the gude Lord thow sall los thy heid.

PAUPER: I sal anis drink or I ga thocht thou had sworne my deid.

Heir Diligence castis away the ledder.

DILIGENCE: Loup now gif thou list for thon hes lost the ledder.

PAUPER: It is full well thy kind to loup and licht in a ledder.
    Thou sal be faine to fetch agane ye ledder or I loup
    I sall sit heir into this tcheir till I haue tumde the stoup.

Heir sall the Carle loup aff the scalfald.

    Swyith begger bogill haist the away,
    Thow art over pert to spill our play.

PAUPER: I wil not gif for al your play worth an sowis fart,
    For thair is richt lytill play at my hungrie hart.

DILIGENCE: Quhat Devill ails this cruckit carle?

PAUPER: Marie meikili sorrow:
   I can not get, thocht I gasp to beg nor to borrow.

DILIGENCE: Quhair deuill is this thou dwels or quhats thy intent?

PAUPER: I dwell into Lawthiane ane myle fra Tranent.

DILIGENCE: Quhair wald thou be carle, the suth to me schaw?

PAUPER: Sir evin to Sanct-Androes for to seik law.

DILIGENCE: For to seik law in Edinburgh was the neirest way,

PAUPER: Sir I socht law thair this monie deir day.
   Bot I cold get nane at Sessioun nor Seinye,
   Thairfoir the mekill din Deuill droun all the meinye.

DILIGENCE: Shaw me thy mater man with al the circumstances.
   How that thou hes happinit on thir unhappie chances.

PAUPER: Gude-man will ye gif me of your Charitie
   And I sall declair yow the black veritie.
   My father was ane auld man and ane hoir,
   And was of age fourscoir of yeirs and moir.
   And Mald my mother was fourscoir and fyfteine,
   And with my labour I did thame baith susteine.
   Wee had ane Meir that caryit salt and coill,
   And everie ilk yeir scho brocht vs hame ane foill.
   VVee had thrie ky that was baith fat and fair,
   Nane tydier into the toun of air.
   My father was sa waik of blude and bane,
   That he deit, quhairfoir my mother maid great maine
   Then scho deit within ane day or two,
   And thair began my povertie and wo.
   Our gude gray Meir was baittand on the feild,
   And our Lands laird tuik hir for his hyreild
   The Vickar tuik the best Cow be the head,
   Incontinent quhen my father was deid.
   And quhen the Vickar hard tel how that my mother.
   Was dead, fra- hand he tuke to him ane uther,
   Then Meg my wife did murne baith evin & morow
   Till at the last scho deit for verie sorow:
   And quhen the Vickar hard tell my wyfe was dead,
   The thrid Cow he cleikit be the head.
   Thair umest clayis that was of rapploch gray,
   The Vickar gart his Clark bear them away.
   Quhen all was gaine I micht mak na debeat
   Bot with my bairns past for till beg my meat.
   Now haue I tald yow the blak veritie,
   How I am brocht into this miserie.

DILIGENCE: How did ye person, was he not thy gude freind?

PAUPER: The devil stick him, he curst me for my teind
    And halds me yit under that same proces
    That gart me want the Sacrament at Pasche.
    In gudefaith sir, thocht he wald cut my throt,
    I haue na geir except ane Inglis grot.
    Quhilk I purpois to gif ane man of law.

DILIGENCE: Thou art the daftest fuill that ever I saw,
    Trows thou man be the law to get remeid,
    Of men of kirk na nocht till thou be deid.

PAUPER: Sir be quhat law tell me quhairfoir or quhy?
    That ane Vickar sould tak fra me thrie ky.

DILIGENCE: Thay haue na law except and consuetude,
    Quhilk law to them is sufficient and gude.

PAUPER: Ane consuetude against the common weill,
    Sould be na law I think besweit Sanct Geill.
    Quhair will ye find that law tell gif ye can?
    To tak thrie ky fra ane pure husband man.
    Ane for my father, and for my wyfe ane uther,
    And the thrid Cow he tuke fra Mald my mother.

DILIGENCE: It is thair law all that thay haue in use
    Thocht it be Cow, Sow, Ganer, Gryse or Guse,

PAUPER: Sir I wald speir at yow ane questioun,
    Behauld sum Prelats of this Regioun,
    Manifestlie during thair lustie lyfis,
    Thay swyfe Ladies, Madinis and uther mens wyfis.
    And sa thair cunts thay haue in consuetude,
    Quhidder say ye that law is evill or gude?

DILIGENCE: Hald thy toung man, it seims that thou war mangit,
    Speik thou of Preists but doubt thou will be hangit.

PAUPER: Be him that buir the cruell Croun of thorne,
    I cair nocht to be hangit evin the morne.

DILIGENCE: Be sure of Preistis thou will get na support,

PAUPER: Gif that be trew the seind resaue the sort.
    Sa sen I se I get na uther grace,
    I will ly doun and rest mee in this place.

Pauper lyis doun in the feild, Pardoner enters.

PARDONER: Bona dies, Bona dies,
    Devoit peopill, gude day I say yow,
    Now tarie ane lytill quhyll I pray yow,

135

Till I be with yow knawin:
Wait ye weill how I am namit?
Ane nobill man and undefamit
Gif all the suith war schawin.
I am sir Robert Rome-raker,
Ane perfite publike pardoner
Admittit be the Paip:
Sirs I sall schaw yow for my wage
My pardons and my pilgramage,
Quhilk ye sall se and graip:
I giue to the deuill with gude intent,
This unsell wickit New-testament.
With them that it translait it:
Sen layik men knew the veritie,
Pardoners gets no charitie,
Without that thay debait it.
Amang the wiues with wrinks and wyles,
As all my marrowis, men begyles,
With our fair fals flattrie:
Yea all the crafts I ken perqueir,
As I was teichit be ane Freir,
Callit Hypocrisie.
Bot now allace, our greit abusioun
Is cleirlie knawin till our confusioun,
That we may sair repent:
Of all credence now I am quyte,
For ilk man halds me at dispyte,
That reids the New-test'ment.
Duill fell the braine that hes it wrocht,
Sa fall them that the Buik hame brocht:
Als I pray to the Rude
That Martin Luther that fals loun,
Black Bullinger and Melancthoun,
Had bene smorde in their cude.
Be him that buir the crowne of thorne,
I wald Sanct Paull had neuer bene borne,
And als I wald his bulks:
VVar never red in the kirk,
Bot amangs freirs into the mirk,
Or riuen amang ruiks.

Heir sall he lay doun his geir upon ane buird and say.

My patent pardouns ye may se,
Cumfra the Caue of Tartarie,
Weill seald with oster-schellis.
Thocht ye haue na contritioun;
Ye sall haue full remissioun

With help of Buiks and bellis.
Heir is ane relict lang and braid,
Of fine Macoull the the richt chaft blaid,
With teith and al togidder:
Of Collings cow heir is ane horne,
For eating of Makconnals corne,
Was slaine into Baquhidder.
Heir is ane coird baith great and lang,
Quhilk hangit Johne the Armistrang,
Of gude hemp soft and sound:
Gude halie peopill I stand for'd,
Quha ever beis hangit with this cord,
Neids never to be dround.
The culum of Sanct Bryds kow,
The gruntill of Sanct Antonis sow,
Quhilk buit his haly bell:
Quha ever he be heiris this bell clinck,
Gif me ane ducat for till drink,
He sall never gang to hell.
Without he be of Baliell borne,
Maisters trow ye that this bescorne?
Cum win this pardoun, cum:
Quha luifis thair wyfis nocht with thair hart
I haue power them for till part,
Me think yow deif and dum.
Hes naine of yow curst wickit wyfis,
That halds yow into sturt and stryfis,
Cum tak my dispensatioun:
Of that cummer I sall mak yow quyte,
How be it your selfis be in the wyte,
And mak ane fals narratioun.
Cum win the pardoun now letse,
For meill, for malt or for monie,
For cok, hen, guse or gryse:
Of relicts heir I haue ane hunder,
Quhy cum ye nocht this is ane wonder?
I trow ye be nocht wyse.

SOWTAR: Welcum hame Robert Rome-raker,
    Our halie patent pardoner:
    Gif ye haue dispensatioun.
    To pairt me and my wickit wyfe,
    And me deliver from sturt and stryfe,
    I mak yow supplicatioun.

PARDONER: I sall yow pairt but mair demand,
    Sa I get mony in my hand,
    Thairfoir let se sum cunye:

SOWTAR: I haue na silver be my lyfe,
    Bot fyue schillings and my schaipping knyfe,
    That sall ye haue but sunye.

PARDONER: Quhat kynd of woman is thy wyfe,

SOWTAR: Ane quick Devill Sir, ane storme of stryfe,
    Ane Frog that fyles the winde:
    Ane fistand flag, a flagartie fuffe,
    At ilk ane pant scho lets ane puffe,
    And hes na ho behind.
    All the lang day scho me dispyts,
    And all the nicht scho flings and flyts,
    Thus sleip I never ane wink:
    That Cockatrice, that commoun huir,
    The mekill Devill may nocht in duir
    Hir stuburnnes and stink.

SOWTARS WYFE: Theif carle thy words I hard rycht weill
    In faith my freindschip ye sall feill,
    And I the fang:

SOWTAR: Gif I said ocht Dame be the Rude,
    Except ye war baith fair and gude,
    God nor I hang.

PARDONER: Fair dame gif ye wald be ane wower,
    To part yow twa I haue ane power,
    Tell on ar ye content?

SOWTARS WYFE: Ye that I am with all my hart
    Fra that fals huirsone till depart,
    Gif this theif will consent.
    Causses to part to part I haue anew,
    Becaus I gat na chamber-glew,
    I tell yow verely
    I meruell nocht, sa mot I lyfe,
    ⌐Howbeit that swingeour can not swyfe,
    He is baith cauld and dry.

PARDONER: Quhat wil ye gif me for your part:

SOWTARS WYFE: Ane cuppill of sarks with all my hart,
    The best claith in the land:

PARDONER: To part sen ye ar baith content,
    I sall yow part incontinent,
    Bot ye mon do command.
    My will and finall sentence is,
    Ilk ane of yow uthers arsse kis:
    Slip doun your hois, me thinkis the carle is glaikit,
    Set thou not by howbeit scho kisse and slaik it,

Heir sall scho kis hir arsse with silence.

Lift up hir dais, kis hir hoill with your hart,

SOWTAR: I pray yow sir forbid hir for to fart.

Heir sall the Carle kis hir arsse with silence.

PARDONER: Dame pas ye to the east end of the toun,
And pas ye west evin lyke ane cuckald loun,
Go hence ye baith with Baliels braid blissing,
Schirs saw ye ever mair sorrowles pairting?

Heir sall the boy cry aff the hill.

WILKIN: Hoaw maister, hoaw, quhalr ar ye now?

PARDONNER: I am heir Wilkin widdie fow.

WILKIN: Sir I haue done your bidding,
For I haue fund ane great hors bane,
Ane fairer saw ye never nane,
Upon Dame Fleschers midding.
Sir, ye may gar the wyfis trow,
It is ane bane of Sanct Bryds cow,
Gude for the feuer quartane:
Sir will ye reull this relict weill,
All the wyfis will baith kis and kneill,
Betuixt this and Dumbartane,

PARDONER: Quhat say thay of me in the toun?

WILKIN: Sum sayis ye ar ane verie loun:
Sum sayis, *Legatus natus:*
Sum sayis y'ar ane fals Saracene,
And sum sayis ye ar for certaine
Diabofus incamatus.
Bot keip yow fra subiectioun,
Of the curst King Correctioun.
For be ye with him fangit:
Becaus ye ar ane Rome-raker,
Ane commoun publick cawsay-paker,
But doubt ye will be hangit.

PARDONER: Quhair sall I ludge into the toun?

WILKIN: With gude kynde Cristiane Anderson,
Quhair ye will be weill treatit
Gif ony li nmer yow demands,
Scho will defend yow with hir hands,
And womanlie debait it.
Bawburdie says be the Trinitie,

> That scho sall beir yow cumpanie,
> Howbeit ye byde ane yeir.

PARDONER: Thou hes done weill be Gods mother
> Tak ye the taine and I the t'other:
> Sa sall we mak greit cheir.

WILKIN: I reid yow speid yow heir,
> And mak na ianger tarie:
> Byde ye lang thair but weir,
> I dreid your weird yow warie.

Heir sall Pauper rise and rax him.

PAUPER: Quhat thing was yon that I hard crak & cry?
> I haue bene dreamand and dreueland of my ky.
> With my richt hand my haill bodie I saine,
> Sanct Bryd, Sanct Bryd, send me my ky againe,
> I se standand yonder ane halie man,
> To mak me help let me se gif he can.
> Halie maister, God speid yow and gude morne,

PARDONER: Welcum to me thocht thou war at the horne,
> Cum win the pardoun and syne I sall the saine,

PAUPER: Will that pardoun get me my ky againe?

PARDONER: Carle of thy ky I haue nathing ado,
> Cum win my my pardon and kis my relicts to.

Heir salt he saine him with his relictis.

PARDONER: Now lows thy pursse & lay doun thy offrand,
> And thou sall haue my pardon euin fra-hand.
> With raipis and relicts I sall the saine againe,
> Of Gut or grauell thou sall neuer haue paine.
> Now win the pardon limmer, or thou art lost:

PAUPER: My haly father quhat wil that pardon cost?

PARDONER: Let se quhat mony thou bearest in thy bag:

PAUPER: I haue ane grot heir bund into ane rag.

PARDONER: Hes thou na uther siluer bot ane groat?

PAUPER: Gif I haue mair sir cum and rype my coat.

PARDONER: Gif me that grot man, gif thou hest na mair.

PAUPER: With all my heart maister lo tak it thair:
> Now let me se your pardon with your leif.

PARDONER: Ane thousand yeir of pardons I the geif.

PAUPER: Ane thousand yeir? I will not Hue sa lang,
    Delyuer me it maister and let me gang.

PARDONER: Ane thousand yeir I lay upon thy head,
    With *tetiens quotiens:* now mak me na mair plead:
    Thou hast resaifit thy pardon now already.

PAUPER: Bot I can se na thing sir be our Lady:
    Forsuith maister, I trow I be not wyse:
    To pay ere I haue sene my marchandryse.
    That ye haue gottin my groat full sair I rew:
    Sir, quhidder is your pardon black or blew?
    Maister, sen ye haue taine fra me my cunyie,
    My marchandryse schaw me withouttin sunyie.
    Or to the Bischop I sall pas and pleinyie
    In Sanct-Androis, & summond yow to the Seinyie.

PARDONER: Quhat craifis the carle me thinks thou art not wise.

PAUPER: I craif my groat or ellis my marchandrise.

PARDONER: I gaif the pardon for ane thowsand yeir,

PAUPER: How sall I get that pardon let me heir?

PARDONER: Stand still and I sall tell the haill storie:
    Quhen thow art deid and gais to Purgatorie,
    Being condempit to paine a thowsand yeir:
    Then sall thy pardoun the releif but weir,
    Now be content – ye ar ane mervelous man:

PAUPER: Sall I get nathing for my grot quhill than?

PARDONER: That sall thou not I mak it to yow plaine.

PAUPER: Na than gossop, gif me my grot againe.
    Quhat say ye maisters call ye this gude resoun?
    That he sould promeis me ane gay pardoun:
    And he resaue my money in his stead,
    Syne mak me na payment till I be dead:
    Quhen I am deid I wait full sikkerlie,
    My sillie saull will pas to Purgatorie:
    Declair me this? now God nor Baliell bind the,
    Quhen I am thair curst carle, quhair sall I find the?
    Not into heavin, bot rather into hell:
    Quhen you art thalr thou can not help thy sel.
    Quhen will thou cum my dolours till abait?
    Or I the find my hippis will get ane hait.
    Trowis thou butchour that I will by blind lambis:
    Gif me my grot the devill dryte in thy gambis.

PARDONER: Suyith stand abak, I trow this man be mangit:
    Thou gets not this carle, thocht you suld be hangit

PAUPER: Gif me my grot weill bund into ane clout,
    Or be Gods breid Robin sall beir ane rout.

Heir sall thay fecht with silence and Pauper sal cast doun the buird, and cast the relicts in the water

DILIGENCE: Quhat kind of dassing is this al day?
    Suyith smaiks out of the the feild, away.
    Into ane presoun put them sone,
    Syne hang them quhen the play is done.

Heir sall Diligence mak his proclamatioun.

DILIGENCE: Famous peopill tak tent and ye sall se
    The thrie estaits of this natioun:
    Cum to the Court with ane strange gravitie,
    Thairfoir I mak yow supplicatioun:
    Till ye haue heard our haill narratioun,
    To keip silence and be patient I pray yow,
    Howbeit we speik be adulatioun,
    Wee sall say nathing bot the suith I say yow.
    Gude verteous men that luifis the veritie,
    I wait thay will excuse our negligence:
    Bot vicious men denude of charitie,
    As feinyeit fals flattrand Saracens.
    Howbeit thay cry on us ane loud vengence,
    And of our pastyme mak ane fals report.
    Quhat may wee do bot tak in patience?
    And us refer unto the faithfull sort.
    Our Lord Iesus Peter nor Paull,
    Culd nocht compleis the peopill all,
    Bot sum war miscontent:
    Howbeit thay schew the veritie,
    Sum said that it war herisie,
    Be thair maist fals iudgement.

Heir sall the thrie estaits cum fra the palyeoun gang and backwart led be thair vyces.

WANTONNES: Now braid benedicite,
    Quhat thing is yon that I se?
    Luke Solace my hart:

SOLACE: Brother Wantonnes quhat thinks thow?
    Yon ar the thrie estaits I trow:
    Gangand backwart.

WANTONNES: Backwart, backwart, out wallaway?
    It is greit schame for them I say,
    Backwart to gang:

    I trow the King Correctloun,
    Man mak ane reformatioun:
    Or it be lang.
    Now let us go and tell the King,

Pausa.

    Sir wee haue sene ane mervelous thing
    Be our judgement:
    The thrie estaits of this Regioun,
    Ar cummand backwart throw this toun,
    To the Parlament-

REX: Backwart, backwart, how may that be?
    Gar speid them haistelie to me:
    In dreid that thay ga wrang:

PLACEBO: Sir I se them yonder cummand,
    Thay will be he heir evin fra hand,
    Als fast as thay may gang.

GUDE-COUNSELL: Sir hald you stil & skar them nocht·
    Till ye persaue quhat be thair thocht,
    And se quhat men them leids:
    And let the King Correctioun,
    Mak ane scharp inquisitioun,
    And mark them be the heids.
    Quhen ye ken the occasioun,
    That maks them sic persuasioun;
    Ye may expell the caus:
    Syne them reforme as ye think best,
    Sua that the Realme may liue in rest,
    According to Gods lawis.

Heir sall the thrie estaits cum and turne thair faces to the King.

SPIRITUALITIE: Gloir, honour, laud triumph and victorie
    Be to your michtie prudent excellence:
    Heir ar we cum all the estaits thrie,
    Readie to mak our dew obedience.
    At your command with humbill observance,
    As my pertene to Spiritualitie.
    With counsell of the Temporalitie.

TEMPOR: Sir we with michtie curage at command
    Of your superexcellent Maiestie,
    Sall mak seruice baith with our hart and hand,
    And sall not dreid in thy defence to die:
    Wee ar content but doubt that wee may se
    That nobill heavinlie King Correctioun,
    Sa he with mercie mak punitioun.

MERCHAND: Sir we ar heir your Burgessis and Merchands,
    Thanks be to God that we may se your face:
    Traistand wee may now into divers lands,
    Convoy our geir with support of your grace.
    For now I traist wee sall get rest and peace,
    Quhen misdoars ar with your sword overthrawin
    Then may leil-merchands liue upon thair awin.

REX: Welcum to me my prudent Lords all,
    Ye ar my members suppois I be your head:
    Sit doun that we may with your just counsall,
    Aganis misdoars find soveraine remeid.
    Wee sall nocht spair for fauour nor for feid,
    With your avice to mak punitioun:
    And put my sword to executioun.

CORRECTIOUN: My tender freinds I pray yow with my hart,
    Declair to me the thing that I wald speir,
    Quhat is the caus that ye gang ail backwart?
    The veritie thair of faine wald I heir.

SPIRITUALITIE: Soveraine we haue gaine sa this mony a yeir
    Howbeit ye think we go undecently,
    Wee think wee gang richt wonder pleasantly.

DILIGENCE: Sit doun my Lords into your proper places:
    Syne let the King consider all sic caces.
    Sit doun sir scribe, and sit doun dampster to:
    And fence the Court as ye war wont to do.

Thay ar set doun & Gude-counsell sal pas to his seat.

REX: My prudent Lords of the thrie estaits,
    It is our will abuife all uther thing,
    For to reforme all them that maks debaits,
    Contrair the richt quhilk daylie dois maling.
    And thay that dois the Common-weil doun thring
    With help and counsell of King Correctioun,
    It is our will for to mak punisching:
    And plaine oppressours put to subiectioun.

SPIRITUALITIE: Quhat thing is this sir, that ye haue devyst
    Schirs ye haue neid for till be weill advysit
    Be nocht haistie into your executioun,
    And be nocht our extreime in your punitioun.
    And gif ye please to do sir, as wee say,
    Postpone this Parlament till ane uther day.
    For quhy? the peopill of this Regioun,
    May nocht indure extreme correctioun.

CORRECTIOUN: Is this the part my Lords that ye will tak,

    To mak us supportatioun to correct:
It dois appeir that ye ar culpabill,
That ar nocht to Correctioun applyabill.
Suyith Diligence gaschaw it is our will,
That everilk man opprest geif in his Bill.

DILIGENCE: All maneir of men I wairne that be opprest,
    Cum and complaine and thay salbe redrest.
    For quhy, it is the nobill Princes will,
    That ilk compleiner sall gif in his Bill.

Johne the Common-weill.

    Out of my gait, for Gods saik let me gae.
    Tell me againe gude maister quhat ye say.

DILIGENCE: I warne al that be wrangouslie offendit,
    Cum and complaine and thay sall be a nendit.

JOHNE: Thankit be Christ yat buir the croun of thorne
    For I was never sa blyth sen I was borne.

DILIGENCE: Quhat is thy name follow – that wald I feil?

JOHNE: Forsuith thay call me Johne the Common-weil.
    Gude maister I wald speir at you ane thing,
    Quhair traist ye I sall, find yon new cumde King?

DILIGENCE: Cum over, and I sall schaw the to his grace,
    Johne – Gods bennesone licht on that luckie face.
    Stand by the gait, let se gif I can loup,
    I man rin fast incace I get ane coup.

Heir sall Johne loup the stank or els fall in it.

DILIGENCE: Speid the away, thou taryis all to lang:

JOHNE: Now be this day I may na faster gang.

Johne to the King.

    Gude day, gud day, grit God saif baith your graces
    Wallie, wallie fall thay twa weill fairde faces.

REX: Shaw me thy name gude man I the command,

JOHNE: Marie Johne the common-weil of fair Scotland

REX: The commoun weill hes bene amang his fais:

JOHNE: Ye sir that gars the commoun-weil want clais.

REX: Quhat is the caus the common weil is crukit?

JOHNE: Becaus the common-weill hes bene overlukit

REX: Quhat gars the luke sa with ane dreirie hart?

JOHNE: Becaus the thrie estaits gangs all backwart.

REX: Sir common weill knaw ye the limmers that then leids?

JOHNE: Thair canker cullours I ken them be the heads –
    As for our reverent fathers of Spiritualitie,
    Thay ar led be Couetice and cairles Sensualitie.
    And as ye se Temporalitie hes neid of correctioun –
    Quhilk hes lang tyme bene led be publick oppressioun –
    Loe quhair the loun lyis lurkand at his back,
    Get up I think to se thy craig gar ane raip crack.
    Loe heir is Falset and Dissait weill I ken,
    Leiders of the merchants and sillie crafts-men.
    Quhat mervell thocht the thrie estaits backwart gang?
    Quhen sic an vyle cumpanie dwels them amang.
    Quhilk hes reulit this rout monie deir dayis,
    Quhilk gars Johne the common-weil want his warme clais
    Sir call them befoir yow and put them in ordour,
    Or els Johne the common-weil man beg on the bordour.
    Thou feinyelt Flattrie the feind fart in thy face,
    Quhen ye was guyder of the Court we gat litill grace.
    Ryse up Falset and Dissait without ony sunye,
    I pray God nor the devils dame dryte on thy grunye.
    Behauld as the loun lukis evin lyke a theif,
    Monie wicht warkman thou brocht to mischeif.
    My soveraine Lord Correction I mak yow supplication,
    Put thir tryit truikers from Christis congregation.

CORRECTIOUN: As ye haue devysit but doubt it sa be done
    Cum heir my Sergeants and do your debt sone.
    Put thir thrie pellours into pressoun Strang,
    Howbeit ye sould hang them ye do them na wrahg.

FIRST SERGEANT: Soverane Lords wee sall obey your commands:
    Brother upon thir limmers lay on thy hands.
    Ryse up sone loun thou luiks evin lyke ane lurden:
    Your mouth war meit to drink an wesche lurden.

SECUND SERGEANT: Cum heir gossop, cum heir, cum heir,
    Your rackles lyfe ye sall repent:
    Quhen was ye wont to be sa sweir?
    Stand still and be obedient.

FIRST SERGEANT: Thair is nocht in all this toun,
    Bot I wald nocht this taill war tald –
    Bot I wald hang him for his goun,
    Quhidder that it war Laird or laid.
    I trow this pellour be spur-gaid,
    Put in thy hand into this cord,

Howbeit I se thy skap skyre skaid:
Thou art ane stewat I stand foird.

Heir sall the vycis be led to the stocks.

SECUND SERGEANT: Put in your leggis into the stocks,
    For ye had never ane meiter hois:
    Thir stewats stinks as thay war Broks,
    Now ar ye sikker I suppois.

Pausa.

    My Lords wee haue done your commands,
    Sall wee put Covetice in captivitie?

CORRECTIOUN: Ye hardlie lay on them your hands,
    Rycht sa upon Sensualitie,

SPIRITUALITIE: This is my Grainter and my Chalmerlaine,
    And hes my gould and geir under hir cuiris:
    I mak ane vow to God I sall complaine,
    Unto the Paip how ye do me iniuris.

COVENCE: My reverent fathers tak in patience,
    I sall nocht lang remaine from your pesence
    Thocht for ane quhyll I man from yow depairt,
    I wait my spreit sall remaine in your hart.
    And quhen this King Correctioun beis absent,
    Then sall we twa returne incontinent.
    Thairfoir adew. –

SPIRITUALITIE: Adew be Sanct Mavene,
    Pas quhair ye will we ar twa naturall men.

SENSUALITIE: Adew my Lord –

SPIRITUALLTIE: Adew my awin sweit hart.
    Now duill fell me that wee twa man depart.

SENSUALITIE: My Lord howbeit this parting dois me paine,
    I traist in God we sal meit sone agane.

SPIRITUALITIE: To cum againe I pray yow do your cure,
    Want I yow twa I may nocht lang indure.

Heir sal the Sergeants chase them away, and they sal gang to the seat of Sensualitie.

TEMPOR: My Lords ye knaw the thrie estaits,
    For Common-weill suld mak debaits:
    Let now amang us be devysit,
    Sic actis that with gude men be praysit.
    Conforming to the common law,

For of na man we sould stand aw.
And for till saif us fra murmell,
Schone Diligence fetch us Gude-counsell
For quhy he is ane man that knawis,
Baith the Cannon and Civill lawis.

DILIGENCE: Father ye man incontinent,
Passe to the Lords of Parliament.
For quhy thay ar determinat all,
To do na thing by your counsall.

GUDE-COUNSELL: That sal I do within schort space,
Praying the Lord to send us grace:
For till conclude or wee depart,
That thay may profeit esterwart,
Baith to the Kirk and to the King,
I sall desyre na uther thing.

Pausa.

My Lords God glaid the cumpanie,
Quhat is the caus ye send for me?

MERCHAND: Sit doun and gif us your counsell,
How we sall slaik the greit murmell,
Of pure peopill, that is weill knawin,
And as the Common-weill hes schawin.
And als wee knaw it is the Kings will,
That gude remeid be put thairtill.
Sir Common-weill keip ye the bar,
Let nane except your self cum nar.

JOHNE: That sall I do as I best can,
I sall hauld out baith wyfe and man –
Ye man let this puir creature,
Support me for till keip the dure.
I knaw his name full sickerly,
He will complaine als weill as I.

GUDE-COUNSELL: My worthy Lords sen ye haue taine on hand
Sum reformatioun to mak into this land:
And als ye knaw it is the Kings mynd,
Quha till the Common-weil hes ay bene kynd:
Thocht reif and thift wer stanchit weill aneuch,
Yit sumthing mair belangis to the pleuch.
Now into peace ye sould provyde for weirs,
And be sure of how mony thowsand speirs,
The King may be quhen he hes ocht ado,
For quhy my Lords this is my ressoun to.
The husband men and commons thay war wont,

Go in the battell formest in the front —
Bot I haue tint all my experience,
Without ye mak sum better diligence:
The Common-weill mon uther wayis be styllit —
Or be my faith the King wilbe begyllit.
Thir pure commouns daylie as ye may se,
Declynisdoun till extreme poverrie:
For sum ar hichtit sa into thair maill,
Thair winning will nocht find them water kaill.
How Prelats heichts thair teinds it is weill knawin,
That husband-men may not weill hald thair awin.
And now begins ane plague amang them new,
That gentill men thair steadings taks in rew.
Thus man thay pay great ferme or lay thair steid,
And sum ar plainlie harlit out be the heid,
And ar distroy it without God on them rew.

PAUPER: Sir be Gods breid that taill is verie trew.
It is weill kend I had baith nolt and hors,
Now all my geir ye se upon my cors.
Correction, Or I depairt I think to mak ane ordour

JOHNE: I pray yow sir begin first at bordour.
For how can we send us aganis Ingland
Quhen we can nocht within our natiue Land,
Destroy our awin Scots, common trator theifis,
Quha to leill laborers daylie dois mischeifis.
War I ane King my Lord be Gods wounds,
Quha ever held common theifis within thair bounds:
Quhairthrow that dayly leilmen micht be wrangit
Without remeid thair chiftanis suld be hangit,
Quhidder he war ane knicht, ane Lord or Laird
The Devill draw me to hell and he war spaird.

TEMPORA: Quhat uther enemies hes thou let us ken?

JOHNE: Sir I compleine upon the idill men:
For quhy sir it is Gods awin bidding
All Christian men to wirk for thair living.
Sanct Paull that pillar of the Kirk,
Sayis to the wretchis that will not wirk
And bene to vertews laith
Qui non laborat non manducet.
This is in Inglische toung or leit:
Quha labouhs nocht he sall not eit.
This bene against the strang beggers,
Fidlers, pypers, and pardoners:
Thir lugglars, lestars, and idill cuitchours,
Thir carriers and thir quintacensours:

149

Thir babil-beirers and thir bairds,
Thir sweir swyngeours with Lords and Lairds:
Ma then thair rents may susteine,
Or to thair profeit neidfull bene,
Quhilk bene ay blythest of discords,
And·deidly feid amang thar Lords.
For then they sleutchers man be treatit –
Or els thair querrels undebaitit.
This bene against thir great fat Freiris,
Augustenes, Carmleits and Cordeleirs:
And all uthers that in cowls bene cled,
Quhilk labours nocht and bene weill fed.
I mein nocht laborand Spirituallie,
Nor for thair living corporallie:
Lyand in dennis lyke idill doggis
I them compair to weil fed hoggis –
I think they do them selfis abuse,
Seing that thay the warld refuse:
Haifing profest sic povertie,
Syne fleis fast fra necessitie.
Quhat gif thay povertie wald professe?
And do as did Diogenes,
That great famous Philosophour,
Seing in earth bot vaine labour,
Alutterlie the warld refusit,
And in ane tumbe him self inclusit,
And leifit on herbs and water cauld,
Of corporall fude na mair he wald.
He trottit nocht from toun to toun,
Beggand to feid his carioun.
Fra tyme that lyfe he did profes,
The wald of him was cummerles.
Rycht sa of Marie Magdalene,
And of Mary th'Egyptiane:
And of auld Paull the first Hermeit,
All thir had povertie compleit.
Ane hundreth ma I micht declair,
Bot to my purpois I will fair:
Concluding sleuthfull idilnes,
Against the Common-weill expresse.

CORRECTIOUN: Quhom upon ma will ye complefne?

JOHNE: Marie on ma and ma againe.
For the pure peopill cryis with cairis,
The infetching of Iustice airis:
Exercit mair for couetice,
Then for the punisching of vyce.
Ane peggrell theif that steillis ane kow,

Is hangit bot he that steillis ane bow
With als meikill geir as he may turs,
That theif is hangit be the purs.
Sic pykand peggrall theifis ar hangit,
Bot he that all the warld hes wrangit,
Ane cruell tyrane ane Strang transgressour,
Ane common publick plaine oppressour,
By buds may he obteine fauours
Of Tresurers and compositeurs.
Thocht he serue greit punitioun,
Gets easie compositioun:
And throch laws consistoriall
Prolixt, corrupt and perpetuall.
The common peopill ar put sa under,
Thocht thay be puir it is na wonder.

CORRECTIOUN: Gude Johne I grant all that is trew –
Your infortoun full sair I rew:
Or I pairt aff this Natioun,
I sall mak reformatioun.
And als my Lord Temporalitie,
I yow command in tyme that ye
Expell oppressioun aff your lands.
And als I say to yow merchands,
Gif ever I find be land or sie,
Dissait be in your cumpanie:
Quhilk ar to Common-weill contrair,
I vow to God I sall not spair
To put my sword to executioun,
And mak on yow extreme punitioun.
Mairover my Lord Spiritualitie,
In gudlie haist I will that ye
Set into few your temporall lands.
To men that labours with thair hands.
Bot nocht to ane gearking gentill man,
That nether will he wirk, nor can:
Quhair throch the policy may incresse.

TEMPORALITIE: I am content sir be the messe:
Swa that the Spiritualitie,
Sets thairs in few als weill as wee.

CORRECTIOUN: My Spirituall Lords ar ye content?

SPIRITUALITIE: Na, na, wee man tak advysement
In sic maters for to conclude,
Ouir haistelie, wee think nocht gude.

CORRECTIOUN: Conclude ye nocht with the Common-weil
Ye salbe punischit be Sanct Geill.

Heir sall the Bischops cum with the Freir.

SPIRITUALITIE: Schir we can schaw exemptioun,
    Fra your temporall punitioun:
    The quhilk wee purpois till debait.

CORRECTIOUN: Wa than, ye think to stryue for stair.
    My Lords quhat say ye to this play?

TEMPORALITIE: My soverane Lords we will obay,
    And tak your part with hart and hand,
    Quhat ever ye pleis us to command.

Heir sall the Temporal stait sit doun on thair knies, & say.

    Bot wee beseik yow Soveraine,
    Of all our cryms that ar bygaine
    To gifvs ane remissioun,
    And heir wee mak to yow conditioun,
    The Common-weill for till defend
    From hence-forth till our liues end.

CORRECTIOUN: On that conditioun I am content
    Till pardon yow sen ye repent,
    The Common-weill tak be the hand.
    And mak with him perpetuall band.

Heir sall the temporal staits, to wit, the Lords and Merchands imbreasse Johne the Common-weill.

    Johne haue ye ony ma debaits
    Against the Lords of Spirituall staits?
    Johne, Na sir I dar nocht speik ane word
    To plaint on Preistis it is na bourd:

CORRECTIOUN: Flyt on thy fow fill I desyre the:
    Swa that thou schaw bot the veritie.

JOHNE: Grandmerces then I sall nocht spair,
    First to compleine on the Vickair.
    The pure Cottar being lyke to die,
    Haifand young infants twa or thrie:
    And hes twa ky but ony ma,
    The Vickar most haif ane of thay:
    With the gray frugge that covers the bed,
    Howbeit the wyse be purelie cled,
    And gif the wyfe die on the morne,
    Thocht all the bairns sould be forlorne,
    The uther kow he cleiks away
    With the pure cot of raploch gray.
    Wald God this custome war put doun,
    Quhilk never was found it be ressoun.

TEMPORALITIE: Ar all thay tails trew that thou telles?

PAUPER: Trew sir, the Divill stick me elles,
    For be the halie Trinitie,
    That same was practeisit on me.
    For our Vickar God giue him pyne,
    Hes yit thrie tydie kye of myne.
    Ane for my father and for my wyfe ane uther,
    And the thrid cow he tuke for Maid my mother.

JOHNE: Our Persone heir he takis na uther pyne,
    Bot to ressaue his teinds and spend them syne.
    Howbeit he be obleist be gude ressoun,
    To preich the Evangell to his parochoun.
    Howbeit thay suld want preiching sevintin yeir.
    Our Persoun will not want ane scheif of beir.

PAUPER: Our bishops with thair lustie rokats quhyte,
    Thay flow in riches royal lie and delyte
    Lyke Paradice bend thair palices and places,
    And wants na pleasour of the fairest faces.
    Als thir Prelates hes great prerogatyues,
    For quhy thay may depairt ay with thair wyues:
    Without ony correctioun or damnage,
    Syne tak ane uther wantoner but manage,
    But doubt I wald think it ane pleasant lyfe,
    Ay on quhen I list to part with my wyfe.
    Syne tak ane uther of far greiter bewtie,
    Bot ever alace my Lords that may not be,
    For I am bund alace in mariage,
    Bot thay lyke rams rudlie in thair rage.
    Unpysalt rinnis amang the sillie yowis,
    Sa lang as kynde of nature in them growis.

PERSONER: Thou lies fals huirsun raggit loun,
    Thair is na Preists in all this toun,
    That ever vsit sic vicious crafts.

JOHNE: the feind ressaue thay flattrand chafts:
    Sir Domine I trowit ye had be dum.
    Quhair Devil gat we this ill fairde blaitie bum?

PERSONER: To speik of Preists be sure it is na bourds;
    Thay will burne men now for rakles words,
    And all thay words ar herisie in deid,

JOHNE: The mekil feind resaue the saul that leid.
    All that I say is trew thocht thou be greifit,
    And that I offer on thy pallet to preif it.

SPIRITUALITIE: My lords quhy do ye thoil that lurdun loun,

Of Kirk-men to speik sic detractioun.
I let yow wit my Lords it is na bourds,
Of Prelats for till speik sic wantoun words.

Heir Spiritualitie fames and rages.

Yon villaine puttis me out of Charitie.

TOMPO: Quhy my Lord, sayis he ocht bot verity
Ye can nocht stop ane pure man for till pleinye
Gif he hes faltit, summond him to your Seinye.

SPIRITUALITIE: Yea that I sall, I mak greit God a vow
He sall repent that he spak of the kow.
I will not suffer sic words of yon villaine.

PAUPER: I han gar gif me my thrie fat ky againe.

SPIRITUALITIE: Fals carle to speik to me stands thou not aw?

PAUPER: The feind resaue them that first devysit that law
Within an houre efter my dade was deid
The Vickar had my kow hard be the heid.

PERSON: Fals huirsun carle I say that law is gude,
Becaus it hes bene lang our consuetude:

PAUPER: Quhen I am Paip that law I sal put doun
It is ane sair law for the pure commoun.

SPIRITUALITIE: I mak an vow thay words thou sal repent.

COUNSELL: I yow requyre my Lords be patient.
Wee came nocht heir for disputatiouns,
Wee came to make gude reformatiouns.
Heirfoir of this your propositioun,
Conclude and put to executioun.

MERCHANT: My Lords conclud that al the temporal lands
Be set in few to laboreris with thait hands.
With sic restrictiouns as sall be devysit,
That thay may liue and nocht to be supprysit.
With ane ressonabill augmentatioun,
And quhen thay heir ane proclamatioun:
That the Kings grace dois mak him for the weit,
That thay be reddie with harneis, bow and speir.
As for my self my Lord this I conclude.

COUNSELL: Sa say we all your ressoun be sa gude.
To mak ane Act on this we ar content.

JOHNE: On that sir Scribe I tak ane instrument.
Quhat do ye of the corspresent and kow?

COUNSELL: I wil conclude nathing of that as now
    Without my Lord of Spiritualitie,
    Thairto consent with all this haill cleargie.
    My Lord Bischop will ye thairto consent?

SPIRITUALITIE: Na, na, never till the day of judgement.
    Wee will want nathing that wee haue in use,
    Kirtil nor kow, teind lambe, teind gryse nor guse.

TEMPORALITIE: Forsuith my lord I think we suldconclude,
    Seing this kow ye haue in consuetude:
    Wee will decerne heir that the Kings grace.
    Sall wryte unto the Paipis holines:
    With his consent be proclamatioun,
    Baith corspresent and cow wee sall cry doun.

SPIRITUALITIE: To that my Lords wee plainlie disassent,
    Noter thair of I tak ane instrument.

TEMPORALITIE: My lord be him that al the warld hes wrocht,
    Wee set nocht by quhider ye consent or nocht:
    Ye ar bot ane estait and we ar twa,
    Et ubi maior pars ibi tota.

JOHNE: My lords ye haif richt prudentlie concludit,
    Tak tent now how the land is clein denudit:
    Of gould and silver quhilk daylie gais to Rome,
    For buds, mair then the rest of Christindome.
    War I ane King sir be coks passioun,
    I sould gar mak ane proclamatioun.
    That never ane penny sould go to Rome at all,
    Na mair then did to Peter nor to Paull.
    Da ye nocht sa, heir for conclusioun
    I gif yow all my braid black malesoun.

MERCHANT: It is of treuth sirs, be my christindome.
    That mekil of our money gais to Rome.
    For we merchants I wait within our bounds,
    Hes furneist Preists ten hundreth thowsand punds.
    For thair flnnance, nane knawis sa weill as wee:
    Thairfoir my Lords devyse sum remedie.
    For throw thir playis and thir promotioun,
    Mair for denners nor for devotioun.
    Sir Symonie hes maid with them ane band,
    The gould of weicht thay leid out of the land.
    The Common-weil, thair throch bein sair opprest
    Thairfoir devyse remeid as ye think best.

COUNSELL: It is schort tyme sen ony benefice,
    Was sped in Rome except greit Bischopries.

Bot now for ane unworthie Vickarage,
Ane Preist will rin to Rome in Pilgramage.
Ane cavell quhilk was never at the scule,
Will rin to Rome and keip ane Bischops mule:
And syne cum hame with mony colorit crack,
With ane buirdin of benefices on his back.
Quhilk bene against the, law ane man alane,
For till posses ma benefices norane.
Thir greit commends I say withoutin faill,
Sould nocht be giuen bot to the blude Royall:
Sa I conclude my Lords and sayis for me,
Ye sould annull all this pluralitie.

SPIRITUALITIE: The Palp hes giuen us dispensatiouns:

COUNSELL: Yea that is be your fals narratiouns.
Thocht the Paip for your pleasour will dispence,
I trow that can nocht cleir your conscience.
Advysemy Lords quhat ye think to conclude,

TEMPORALITIE: Sir be my faith I think it verie gude,
That fra hence furth na Preistis sall pas to Rome.
Becaus our substance thay do stillconsume.
For pleyis and for thair profeit singulair,
Thay haif of money maid this realme bair.
And als I think it best be my advyse,
That ilk Preist sall haif bot ane benefice.
And gif thay keip nocht that fundatioun,
It sall be caus of deprivatioun.

MERCHANT: As ye haif said my Lord we wil consent,
Scribe mak ane act on this incontinent.

COUNSELL: My Lords, thair is ane thing yit unproponit
How Prelats and Preistis aucht to be disponit:
This beand done wee haue the les ado;
Quhat say ye sirs- this is my counsall lo:
That or wee end this present Parliament,
Of this mater to tak rype advysement.
Mark weill my Lords, thair is na benefice
Giuen to ane man, bot for ane gude office.
Quha taks office and syne thay can nocht usit,
Giuer and taker I say ar baith abusit.
Ane Bischops office is for to be ane preichour,
And of the law of God ane publick teachour.
Rycht sa the Persone unto his parochoun,
Of the Evangell sould leir them ane lessoun.
Thair sould na man desyre sic dignities,
Without he be abill for that office.

And for that caus, I say without leising,
Thay haue thair teinds, and for na uther thing.

SPIRITUALITIE: Friend quhair find ye that we suld prechours be

COUNSELL: Luik quhat Sanct Paul wryts unto Timothie
Tak thair the Buik let se gif ye can spell.

SPIRITUALITIE: I never red that, thairfoir reid it your sel.

Counsall sall read thir wordis on ane Buik.

Fidelis sermo, siquis Episcopatum desiderat, bonum opus desiderat, oportet eum irreprehensibilem esse, vnius vxoris virum, sobrium, prudentem, ornatum, pudicum, hospitalem, doctorem: non vinelentum, non percussorem: sed modestum.

That is

This is a true saying, If any man desire the office of a Bishop, he desireth a worthie worke: A Bishop therefore must be unproueable, the husband of one wife, &c.

SPIRITUALITIE: Ye temporall men be him that heryit hell,
Ye ar ovir peart with sik maters to mell.

TEMPORALITIE: Sit still my Lord, ye neid not for til braull,
Thir ar the verie words of th'Apostill Paull.

SPIRITUALITIE: Sum sayis be him that woare the croun of thorne,
It had bene gude that Paull had neir bene borne.

COUNSELL: Bot ye may knaw my Lord Sanct Pauls intent,
Schir red ye never the New testament?

SPIRITUALITIE: Na sir, be him that our Lord Jesus sauld,
I red never the New testament nor auld.
Nor ever thinks to do sir be the Rude,
I heir freiris say that reiding dois na gude.

COUNSELL: Till yow to reid them I think it is na lack,
For anis I saw them baith bund on your back:
That samin day that ye was consecrat,
Sir, quhat meinis that?

SPIRITUALITIE: The feind stick them that wat.

MERCHANT: Then befoir God how can ye be excusit?
To haif ane office and waits not how to us it.
Quhairfoir war gifin yow all the temporal lands?
And all thir teinds ye haif amang your hands.
Thay war giuin yow for uther causses I weine,
Nor mummil matins and hald your clayis cleine.
Ye say to the Appostils that ye succeid,

157

Bot ye schaw nocht that into word nor deid.
The law is plaine – our teinds suld furnisch teichours:

COUNSELL: Yea that it sould, or susteine prudent preichours.

PAUPER: Sir God nor I be stickit with ane knyfe,
Gif ever our Persoun preichit in all his lyfe.

PERSONE: Quhat devil raks the of our preiching undocht?

PAUPER: Think ye that ye suld haue the teinds for nocht?

PERSONE: Trowis thou to get remeid carle of that thing?

PAUPER: Yea be Gods breid richt sone war I ane King.

PERSONE: Wald thou of Prelats mak deprivatioun?

PAUPER: Na I suld gar them keip thair fundatioun,
Quhat devill is this, quhom of sould Kings stand aw?
To do the thing that thay sould be the law.
War I ane King be coks deir passioun,
I sould richt sone mak reformatioun.
Failyeand thairof your grace sould richt sone finde,
That Preists sall leid yow lyke ane bellie blinde –

JOHNE: Quhat gif King David war leiuand in thir dayis?
The quhilk did found sa mony gay Abayis:
Or out of heavin quhat gif he luikit doun?
And saw the great abominatioun:
Amang thir Abesses and thir Nunries,
Thair publick huirdomes and thair harlotries,
He wald repent he narrowit sa his bounds,
Of yeirlie rent thries coir of thowsand pounds.
His successours maks litill ruisse I ges,
Of his devotioun or of his holines.

ABBASSE: How dar thou carle presume for to declair,
Or for to mell the with sa heich a mater?
For in Scotland thair did yit never ring,
I let the wit ane mair excellent King.
Of holines he was the verie plant,
And now in heavin he is ane michtfull Sanct.
Becaus that fyftein Abbasies he did found,
Quhair throw great riches hes ay done abound
Into our Kirk and daylie yit abunds,
Bot kings now I trow few Abbasies founds.
I dar weill say thou art condempnit in hel,
That dois presume with sic maters to mell.
Fals huirsun carle thou art ovir arrogant,
To judge the deids of sic ane halie Sanct.

JOHNE: King Iames the first Roy of this Regioun,
    Said that he was ane sair Sanct to the croun.
    I heir men say that the was sumthing blind,
    That gaue away mair nor he left behind.
    His successours that halines did repent,
    Quhilk gart them do great inconvenient.

ABBASSE: My Lord Bishop I mervel how that ye,
    Suffer this carle for to speik heresie?
    Forbe my faith my Lord will ye tak tent,
    He servis for to be brunt incontinent.
    Ye can nocht say bot it is heresie,
    To speik against our law and libertie.

SPIRITUALITIE: *Sancte pater* I mak yow supplicatioun,
    Exame yon carle, syne mak his dilatioun:
    I mak ane vow to God omnipotent,
    That bystour salbe brunt incontinent.
    Venerabill father I sall do your command,
    Gif he seruis deid I sall sune understand.

Pausa.

    Fals huirsun carle schaw furth thy faith,

JOHNE: Me think ye speik as ye war wraith,
    To yow I will nathing declair,
    For ye ar nocht my ordinair.

SPIRITUALITIE: Quhom in trowis thou fals monster mangit?

JOHNE: I trow to God to se the hangit:
    War I ane King be coks passioun,
    I sould gar mak ane congregatioun,
    Of all the freirs of the four ordouris,
    And mak yow vagers on the bordouris,
    Schir will ye giue me audience.
    And I sall schaw your excellence:
    Sa that your grace will giue me leife
    How into God that I beleife.

CORRECTIOUN: Schaw furth your faith and fein ye nocht.

JOHNE: I beleife in God that all hes wrocht,
    And creat everie thing of nocht.
    And in his Son our Lord Jesu,
    Incarnat of the Virgin trew:
    Quha under Pilat tholit passioun,
    And deit for our Salvatioun.
    And on the thrid day rais againe,
    As halie scriptour schawis plane.
    And als my Lord it is weill kend,

How he did to the heavin ascend:
And set him doun at the richt hand,
Of God the father I understand.
And sall cum iudge on Dumisday,
Quhat will ye mair sir that I say?

CORRECTIOUN: Schaw furth the rest, this is na game.

JOHNE: I trow Sanctam Ecclesiam,
Bot nocht in thir Bischops nor thir Freirs,
Quhilk will for purging of thir neirs.
Sard up the ta raw and doun the uther,
The mekill Devill resaue the fidder.

CORRECTIOUN: Say quhat ye will sirs be Sanct Tan,
Me think Johne ane gude Christian man.

TEMPORALITIE: My Lords let be your disputatioun,
Conclude with firme deliberaioun.
How Prelats fra thyne sall be disponit.

MERCHANT: I think for me evin as ye first proponit.
That the Kings grace sall gif na benefice,
Bot till ane peichour that can use that office.
The sillie sauls that bene Christis scheip,
Sould nocht be givin to gormand wolfis to keip.
Quhat bene the caus of all the heresies,
Bot the abusioun of the prelacies?
Thay will correct and will nocht be correctit:
Thinkand to na prince thay will be subiectit.
Quhairfoir I can find na better remeid,
Bot that thir kings man take it in thair heid.
That thair be giuen to na man bischopries,
Except thay preich out throch thair diosies.
And ilk persone priech in his parochon,
And this I say for finall conclusion.

TEMPORALITIE: Wee think your counsall is verie gude,
As ye haue said wee all conclude.
Of this conclusioun Noter wee mak ane act:

SCRYBE: I wryte all day bot gets never ane plack.

PAUPER: Och, my Lords for the halie Trinitie,
Remember to reforme the consistorie,
It hes mair neid of reformatioun,
Nor Ploutois court sir be coks passioun.

PERSONE: Quhat caus hes thou fals pellour for to pleinfye
Quhair was ye ever summond to thair seinye?

PAUPER: Marie I lent my gossop my mear to fecth hame coills
And he hir drounit into the querrell hollis.
And I ran to the Consistorie for to pleinye,
And thair I happinit amang ane greidie meinye.
Thay gaue me first ane thing thay call citandum,
Within aucht dayis I gat bot lybellandum,
Within ane moneth I gat ad opponendum,
In half ane yeir I gat interloquendum,
And syne I gat, how call ye it? ad replicandum:
Bot I could never ane word yit understand him.
And than thay gart me cast out many plackis,
And gart me pay for four and twentie actis.
Bot or thay came half gait to concludendum,
The feind ane plack was left for to defend him.
Thus thay postponit me twa yeir with thair traine,
Syne hodie ad octo bad me cum againe.
And than thir ruiks thay roupit wonder fast,
For sentence silver thay cry it at the last.
Of pronunciandum thay maid me wonder faine,
Bot I gat never my gude gray meir againe.

TEMPORALITIE: My Lords we mon reforme thir consistory lawis,
Quhais great defame aboue the heavins blawis.
I wist ane man in persewing ane kow,
Or he had done he spendit half ane bow.
Sa that the kings honour wee may avance,
Wee will conclude, as thay haue done in France.
Let Sprituall maters pas to Spritualitie,
And Temporall maters to Temporalitie.
Quha failyeis of this sall cost them of thair gude,
Scribe mak ane act, for sa wee will conclude.

SPIRITUALITIE: That act my Lords plainlie I will declait,
It is again is our profeit singulair.
Wee will nocht want our profeit be Sanct Geill.
Temporalitie your profeit is against the Common weil
It salbe done my Lords as ye haue wrocht,
We cure nocht quhidder ye consent or nocht.
Quhairfoir servis then all thir Temporall Judges?
Gif temporall maters sould seik at yow refuges.
My Lord ye say that ye ar Sprituall,
Quhairfoir mell ye than with things temporall?
As we haue done conclude sa sall it stand,
Scribe put our Acts in ordour evin fra hand.

SPIRITUALITIE: Till all your acts plainlie I disassent,
Notar thairof I tak ane instrument.

Heir sall Veritie and Chastitie mak thair plaint at the bar.

VERITIE: My Soverane I beseik your excellence,
    Use justice on Spritualitie:
    The quhilk to us hes done great violence,
    Becaus we did rehers the veritie.
    Thay put us close into Captivitie,
    And sa remanit into subiectioun:
    Into great langour and calamitie,
    Till we war fred be King Correctioun.

CHASTITIE: My lord I haif great caus for to complaine,
    I could get na ludging intill this land:
    The Spirituall stait had me sa at disdane,
    With Dame Sensuall thay haue maid sic ane band.
    Amang them all na freindschip sirs I fand,
    And quhen I came the nobill innis amang,
    My lustie Ladie Priores fra hand:
    Out of hir do rtour durlie scho me dang.

VERITIE: With the advyse sir of the Parliament,
    Hairtlie we mak yow supplicatioun:
    Cause King Correctioun tak incontinent,
    Of all this sort examinatioun.
    Gif thay be digne of deprivatioun,
    Ye haue power for to correct sic cases:
    Chease the maist cunning Clerks of this natioun,
    And put mair prudent pastours in thair places.
    My prudent Lords I say that pure craftsmen,
    Abufe sum Prelats ar mair for to commend:
    Gar exame them and sa ye sall sune ken,
    How thay in vertew Bischops dois transcend.

SCRYBE: Thy life and craft mak to thir Kings kendr
    Quhat craft hes thow deciair that to me plaine?

TAYLOUR: Ane tailyour sir that-can baith mak and mend,
    I wait nane better into Dumbartane.

SCRYBE: Quhairfoir of tailyeours beirs thou the styl?

TAYLOUR: Becaus I wait is nane within ane myll,
    Can better use that craft as I suppois:
    For I can mak baith doublit coat and hois.

SCRYBE: How cal thay you sir with the schaiping knife?

SOWTAR: Ane sowtar sir, nane better into Fyfe.

SCRYBE: Tel me quhairfoir ane sowtar ye ar namit?

SOWTAR: Of that surname I neld nocht be aschamit.
    For I can mak schone brotekins and buittis,
    Gif me the coppie of the Kings cuittis.

And ye sall se richt sune quhat I can do:
Heir is my lasts and weill wrocht ledder lo.

COUNSELL: O Lord my God this is an mervelous thing
How sic misordour in this Realme sould ring.
Sowtars and tailye ours thay ar far mair expert
In thair pure craft and in thair handie art,
Nor ar our Prelatis in thair vocatioun:
I pray yow sirs mak reformatioun.

VERITIE: Alace, alace, quhat gars thir temporal Kings
Into the Kirk of Christ admit sic doings?
My Lords for lufe of Christs passioun,
Of thir ignorants mak depriuatioun.
Quhilk in the court can-do bot flatter and fleich,
And put into thair places that can preich.
Send furth and seik sum devoit cunning Clarks,
That can steir up the peopill to gude warks.

CORRECTIOUN: As ye haue done, Madame I am content,
Hoaw Diligence pas hynd incontinent.
And seik out throw all towns and cities:
And visie all the universities.
Bring us sum Doctours of Divinitie.
With licents in the law and Theoiogie.
With the maist cunning Clarks in all this land,
Speid sune your way and bring them heir fra hand.

DILIGENCE: Quhat gif I find sum halie provinciall?
Or minister of the gray freiris all?
Or ony freir that can preich prudentlie,
Sall I bring them with me in cumpanie?

CORRECTIOUN: Cair thou nocht quhat estait sa ever he be,
Sa thay can teich and preich the veritie,
Maist cunning Clarks with us is best beluifit,
To dignitie thay salbe first promuifit.
Quhidder thay be Munk, Channon, Preist or Freir,
Sa thay can preich faill nocht to bring them heir.

DILIGENCE: Than fair-weill sir, for I am at the flicht,
I pray the Lord to send yow all gude nicht.

Heir sall Diligence pas to the palyeoun.

TEMPORALITIE: Sir we beseik your soverane celsitude,
Of our dochtours to haue compassioun:
Quhom wee may na way marie be the Rude,
Without wee mak sum alienatioun
Of our land for thair supportatioun,
For quhy? the markit raisit bene sa hie

163

That Prelats dochtours of this natioun,
Ar maryit with sic superfluitie:
Thay will nocht spair to gif twa thowsand pound,
With thair dochtours to ane nobill man:
In riches sa thay do superabound.
Bot we may nocht do sa be Sanct Allane,
Thir proud Prelats our dochters sair may ban;
That thay remaine at hame sa lang unmaryit:
Schir let your Barrouns do the best thay can,
Sum of our dochtours I dreid salbe miscaryit.

CORRECTIOUN: My Lord your complaint is richt ressonabill,
And richt sa to our dochtours profitabill:
I think or I pas aff this natioun,
Of this mater till mak reformatioun.

Heir sall enter common thift.

THIFT: Gae by the gait man, let me gang,
How Devill came I into this thrang:
With sorrow I may sing my sang,
And I be taine:
For I haue run baith nicht and day,
Throw speid of fut I gat away,
Gif I be kend heir, wallaway
I will be slaine.

PAUPER: Quhat is thy name man be thy thrift?

THIFT: Huirsun thay call me common thift:
For quhy I had na uther schift,
Sen I was borne,
In Eusdaill was my dwelling place,
Mony ane wyfe gart I cry alace:
At my hand thay gat never grace,
Bot ay for lorne.
Sum say is ane king is cum amang us,
That purposis to head and hang us:
Thair is na grace gif he may fang us
Bot on an pin.
Ring he, we theifiswill get na gude,
I pray God and the halie Rude,
He had bene smoird into his cude,
And all his kin.
Get this curst King me in his grippis,
My craig will wit quhat weyis my hippist
The Devill I gif his toung and lippis,
That of me tellis:
Adew I dar na langer tarie:

For be I kend thay will me carie,
And put me in ane sierie farie,
I se nocht ellis.
I raife be him that herryit hell,
I had almaist foryet my sell:
Will na gude fallow to me tell,
Quhair I may finde
The Earle of Rothus best haiknay,
That was my earand heir away:
He is richt starck as I heir say
And swift as winde.
Heir is my brydill and my spurris,
To gar him lance ovir land and furris:
Micht I him get to Ewis durris, I tak na cuir:
Of that hors micht I get ane sicht,
I haife na doubt yit or midnicht,
That he and I sould tak the flicht
Throch Dysert mure.
Of cumpanarie tell me brother,
Quhilk is the richt way to the Strother,
I wald be welcum to my mother,
Gif I micht speid:
I wald gif baith my coat and bonet,
To get my Lord Lindesay is broun Jonet:
War he beyond the watter of Annet,
We sould nocht dreid.
Quhat now Oppressioun my maister deir?
Quhat mekill Devill hes brocht yow heir?
Maister tell me the caus perqueir,
Quhat is that ye haue done?

OPPRESSIOUN: Forsuith the kings maiestie,
Hes set me heir as ye may se:
Micht I speik Temporalitie,
He wald me releife sone.
I beseik yow my brother deir,
Bot halfe ane houre for to sit heir:
Ye knaw that I was never sweir,
Yow to defend:
Put in your leg into my place,
And heir I sweir be Gods grace,
Yow to releife within schort space,
Syne let yow wend.

THIFT: Than maister deir gif me your hand,
And mak to me ane faithfull band,
That ye sall cum agane fra hand
Withoutin faill.

165

OPPRESSIOUN: Tak thair my hand richt faithfullie
    Als I promit the verelie,
    To gif to the ane cuppiil of kye
    In Liddisdaill.

Thift puts his legs in the stockis.

    Haif I nocht maid ane honest schift,
    That hes betrasit common Thift?
    For thair is nocht under the lift,
    Ane curster cors:
    I am richt sure that he and I,
    Within this halyeir craftely
    Hes stolne ane thowsand scheip and ky,
    By meiris and hors.
    Wald God I war baith sound and haill,
    Now liftit into Liddisdaill
    The Mers sould find me beif and kaill,
    Quhat rak of bread:
    War I thair liftit with my lyfe,
    The Devill sould stick me with ane knyfe
    And ever I come againe to Fyfe,
    Quhill I war dead.
    Adew I leife the Devill amang yow,
    That in his fingers he may fang yow:
    With all leill men that dois belang yow,
    For I may rew:
    That ever I came into this land,
    For quhy ye may weill understand,
    I gat na geir to turne my hand:
    Yit anis adew.

Heir sall Diligence conuoy the thrie Clarks.

DILIGENCE: Sir, I haue brocht unto your Excellence,
    Thir famous Clarks of greit intelligence:
    For to the common peopill thay can preich,
    And in the Scuilis in Latine toung can teich,
    This is ane Doctour of Divinitie,
    And thir twa Licents men of gravitie.
    I heare men say thair conversatioun,
    Is maist in Divine Contemplatioun,

DOCTOUR: Grace, peace and rest from the hie Trinitie,
    Mot rest amang this godlie cumpanie:
    Heir ar we cumde as your obedients,
    For to fulfill your just commandements.
    Quhat euir it please your Grace us to command,
    Sir, it sall be obeyit euin fra-hand.

REX: Gud freinds ye ar richt welcome to us all,
    Sit doun all thrie and geif vs your counsall.

CORRECTIOUN: Sir I giue yow baith counsal & command,
    In your office use exercitioun:
    First that ye gar search out throch all your land,
    Quha can nocht put to executioun
    Thair office efter the institutioun,
    Of godlie lawis, conforme to thair vocatioun:
    Put in thair places men of gude conditioun,
    And this ye do without dilatioun.
    Ye ar the head sir of this congregatioun,
    Preordinat be God omnipotent:
    Quhilk hes me send to mak yow supportatioun,
    Into the quhilk I salbe diligent.
    And quha saever beis inobedient,
    And will nocht suffer for to be correctit,
    Thay salbe all deposit incontinent,
    And from your presence they sall be deiectit.

COUNSALL: Begin first at the Spritualitie,
    And tak of them examinatioun,
    Gif they can use their divyne dewetie,
    And als I mak yow supplicatioun,
    All thay that hes thair offices misusit,
    Of them make haistie depriuatioun:
    Sa that the peopill be na mair abusit.

CORRECTIOUN: Ye ar ane Prince of Spritualitie.
    How haue ye usit your office now let se?

SPIRITUALITIE: My lords quhen was thair ony Prelats wont,
    Of thair office till ony King mak count?
    Bot of my office gif ye wald haue the feill,
    I let yow wit I haue it usit weill.
    For I tak in my count twyse in the yeir,
    Wanting nocht of my teind ane boll of beir.
    I gat gude payment of my Temporall lands,
    My buttock-maill, my coattis and my offrands,
    With all that dois perteine my benefice,
    Consider now my Lord gif I be wyse.
    I dar nocht marie contrair the common law,
    Ane thing thair is my Lord that ye may knaw.
    Howbeit I dar nocht plainlie spouse ane wyfe,
    Yit Concubeins I haue had four or fyfe.
    And to my sons I haue giuin rich rewairds,
    And all my dochters maryit upon lairds.
    I let yow wit my Lord I am na fuill,
    For quhy I ryde upon ane amland Muill.

Thair is na Temporall Lord in all this land,
That makssic cheir I let yow understand.
And als my Lord I gif with gude intentioun,
To divers Temporall Lords ane yeirlie pensioun
To that intent that thay with all thair hart,
In richt and wrang sal plainlie tak my part.
Now haue I tauld yow sir on my best ways,
How that I haue exercit my office.

CORRECTIOUN: I weind your office had bene for til preich,
And Gods law to the peopill teich,
Quhalrfoir weir ye that mytour ye me tell?

SPIRITUALITIE: I wat nocht man be him that herryit hel

CORRECTIOUN: That dois betakin that ye with gude intent,
Sould teich & preich the auld & New testament

SPIRITUALITIE: I haue ane freir to preiche into my place,
Of my office ye heare na mair quhill Pasche.

CHASTITIE: My Lords this Abbot and this Priores
Thay scorne thair gods, this is my reason quhy,
Thay beare an habite of feinyeit halines,
And in thair deid thay do the contrary:
For to Hue chaist thay vow solemnitly,
Bot fra that thay be sikker of thair bowis
Thay liue in huirdome and in harlotry,
Examine them Sir, how thay obserue thair vowis.

CORRECTIOUN: Sir Scribe ye sall at Chastities requeist
Pas and exame yon thrie in gudlie haist.

SCRYBE: Father Abbot this counsall bids me speir,
How ye haue usit your Abbay thay wald heir.
And als thir Kings hes giuin to me commissioun,
Of your office for to mak inquisitioun.

ABBOT: Tuiching my office I say to yow plainlie,
My Monks and I, we leif richt easelie:
Thair is na Monks from Carrick to Carraill
That fairs better and drinks mair helsum Ailt.
My Prior is ane man of great devotioun,
Thairfoir daylie he gets ane double portioun.

SCRYBE: My Lords how haue ye keipt your thrie vows

ABBASSE: Indeid richt weill till I gat hame my bows.
In my Abbay quhen I was sure professour,
Then did I leife as did my predecessour.
My paramours is baith als fat and fair,
As ony wench into the toun of Air.

    I send my sons to Pareis to the scullis,
    I traist in God that thay salbe na fuillis,
    And all my douchters I haue weill providit,
    Now judge ye gif my office be weill gydit.

SCRYBE: Maister Person schaw us gif ye can preich?

PERSONE: I preich not I can play at the caiche:
    I wait thalr is nocht ane amang yow all,
    Mair ferilie can play at the fut ball:
    And for the carts the tabils and the dyse,
    Aboue all persouns I may beir the pryse.
    Our round bonats we mak them now four nuickit
    Of richt fyne stuiff gif yow list cum and luikit.
    Of my office I haue declarit to the,
    Speir quhat ye pleis, ye get na mair of me.

SCRYBE: Quhat say ye now my Ladie Priores?
    How haue ye usit your office can ye ges?
    Quhat was the caus ye refusit harbrie?
    To this young lustie Ladie Chastitie.

PRIORES: I wald haue harborit hir with gude intent,
    Bot my complexioun thairto wald not assent:
    I do my office efter auld use and wount,
    To your Parliament I will mak na mair count.

VERITIE: Now caus sum of your cunning Clarks
    Quhilk ar expert in heavinlie warks,
    And men fulfill it with charitie
    That can weill preiche the veritie,
    And gifto sum of them command
    Ane sermon for to make fra-hand.

CORRECTIOUN: As ye haue said I am content,
    To gar sum preich incontinent,

Pausa.

    Magister noster I ken how ye can teiche,
    Into the scuillis and that richt ornatlie:
    I pray yow now that ye wald please to preiche,
    In Inglisch toung, land folk to edifie.

DOCTOUR: Soverane I sall obey yow humbillie,
    With ane schort sermon presentlie in this place:
    And schaw the word of God unfeinyeitlie,
    And sinceirlie as God will giue me grace.

Heir sall the Doctour pas to the pulpit and say.

    Si vis ad vitam ingredi serva mandata.

Devoit peopill Sanct Paull the preichour sayis,
The fervent luife and father lie pitie,
Quhilk God almichtie hes schawin mony wayis
To man in his corrupt fragilitie,
Exceids all luife in earth, sa far that we
May never to God mak recompence conding
As quhasa lists to reid the veritie,
In halie Scripture he may find this thing.
Sic Deus dilexit mundum.

Tuiching nathing the great prerogatiue,
Quhilk God to man in his creatioun lent:
How man of nocht creat superlatiue
Was to the Image of God omnipotent
Let us consider that speciall luife ingent,
God had to man quhen our foir-father fell,
Drawing us all in his loynis immanent,
Captive from gloir in thirlage to the hel.
Quhen Angels fell, thair miserabil ruyne
Was never restorit: bot for our miserie,
The Sun of God secund persone divyne,
In ane pure Virgin tuke humanitie:
Syne for our saik great harmis suffered he
In fasting, walking, in preiching, cauld and heit,
And at the last ane schamefull death deit he,
Betwix twa theifis on Croce he yeild the Spreit:
And quhair an drop of his maist precious blude
Was recompence sufficient and conding,
Ane thowsand warlds to ransoun from that wod
Infernall feind, Sathan, notwithstanding
He luifit us sa, that for our ransoning,
He sched furth all the blude of his bodie,
Riven rent and sair wondit quhair he did hing,
Naild on the Croce on the Mont Calvary.
Et copiosa apud eum redemptio.

O cruell death, be the the venemous
Dragon, the Devill infernall lost his pray:
Be the the stinkand, mirk, contageous,
Deip pit of hell mankynd escaipit fray.
Be the the port of Paradice alsway
Was patent maid unto the heavin sa hie:
Opinnit to man and maid ane reddie way,
To gloir eternall with th'haly Trinitie.
And yit for all thisluife incomparabill,
God askis na rewaird fra us againe
Bot luife for luife: in his command but fabill,
Conteinit ar all haill the lawis ten:

Baith ald and new and commandements ilk ane,
Luife bene the ledder quhilk hes bot steppis twa:
Be quhilk we may clim up to lyfe againe,
Out of this vaill of miserie and wa.
*Diliges Dominum Deum tuum ex toto corde tuo & proxi|mum tuum sicut
teipsum: in his duobus mandatis. &c.*

The first step suithlie of this ledder is,
To luife thy God as the fontaine and well
Of luife and grace: and the secund I wis,
To luife thy nichtbour as thou luifis thy sell,
Quha tynis ane stop of thir twa gais to hel,
Bot he repent and turne to Christ anone,
Hauld this na fabill, the halie Evangell
Bears in effect thir words everie one.
Si vis ad vitam ingredi serva mandata Dei.

Thay tyne thir steps all thay quha ever did sin
In pryde, invy, in ire and lecherie:
In covetice or ony extreme win,
Into sweirnes or into gluttonie.
Or quha dois nocht the deids of mercie,
Gif hungrie meit and gif the naikit clayis.

PERSONE: Now walloway thinks thou na schame to lie,
I trow the Devill a word is trew thou sayis:
Thou sayis thair is bot twa steppis to the heavin
Quha failyeis them man backwarts fall in hell,
I wait it is ten thowsand mylis and sevin
Gif it be na mair, I do it upon thy sell.
Schort leggit men I se be Bryds bell,
Will nevir cum thair, thay steppis bene sa wyde:
Gif thay be the words of the Evangell,
The Sprituall men hes mister of ane gyde.

ABBOT: And I beleif that cruikit men and blinde,
Sall neuer get up upon sa hich ane ledder:
By my gude faith I dreid to ly behinde,
Without God draw me up into ane tedder.
Quhat and I fal, than I will break my bledder:
And I cum thair this day the Devill speid me:
Except God make me lichter nor ane fedder,
Or send me doun gude Widcok wingis to file.

PERSONE: Cum doun dastart and gang sell draiff,
I understand nocht quhat thow said.
Thy words war nather corne nor caiff,
I wald thy toung againe war laide,
Quhair thou sayis pryde is deidlie sin,
I say pryde is bot honestie.

And Covetice of warldlie win
Is bot wisdome, I say for me.
Ire, hardines and gluttonie,
Is nathing ellis but lyfis fude:
The naturall sin of lecherie
Is bot trew luife, all thir ar gude.

DOCTOUR: God and the Kirk hes giuin command,
That all gude Christian men refuse them:

PERSONE: Bot war thay sin I understand,
We men of Kirk wald never use them.

DOCTOUR: Brother I pray the Trinitie,
Your faith and charitie to support:
Causand yow knaw the veritie,
That ye your subiects may comfort.
To your prayers peopill I recommend,
The rewlars of this nobill regioun:
That our Lord God his grace mot to them send,
On trespassours to mak punitioun.
Prayand to God from feinds yow defend,
And of your sins to gif yow full remissioun:
I say na mair, to God I yow commend.

Heir Diligence spyis the freir round and to the Prelate.

DILIGENCE: My lords, I persaue that the Sprituall stait,
Be way of deid purpois to mak debait:
For be the counsall of yon flattrand freir,
Thay purpois to mak all this toun on steir.

FIRST LICENT: Traist ye that thay wilbe inobedient,
To that quhilkis – decreitit in Parliament?

DILIGENCE: Thay se the Paip with awfull ordinance
Makis weir against the michtie King of France:
Richt sa thay think that prelats suld nocht sunyie
Be way of deid defend thair patrimonie.

FIRST LICENT: I pray the brother gar me understand,
Quhair ever Christ possessit ane fut of land.

DILIGENCE: Yea that he did father withoutin fail,
For Christ Jesus was King of Israeli.

FIRST LICENT: I grant that Christ was king abuse al kings
Bot he mellit never with temporall things:
As he hes plain lie done declair him sell,
As thou may reid in his halie Evangell.
Birds hes thair nests, and tods hes thair den,
Bot Christ Jesus the Saviour of men

In ail this warld hes nocht ane penny braid,
Quhair on he may repois his heavinlie head.

DILIGENCE: And is that trew? –
Yes brother be Alhailows;
Christ Jesus had na propertie bot the gallows.
And left not quhen he yeildit up the Spreit,
To by himself ane simpill winding scheit.

DILIGENCE: Christs successours I understand,
Thinks na schame to haue temporall land.
Father thay haue na will I yow assure,
In this warld to be indigent and pure:
Bot sir sen ye ar callit sapient,
Declair to me the caus with trew intent,
Quhy that my lustie Ladie Veritie,
Hes nocht bene weill treatit in this cuntrie?

BATCHELER: Forsuith quhair Prelats uses the counsall
Of beggand freirs in monie regioun,
And thay Prelats with Princes principall,
The veritie but doubt is trampit doun.
And Common-weill put to confusioun.
Gif this be trew to yow I me report:
Thairfoir my Lords mak reformatioun,
Or ye depart hairtlie I yow exhort:
Sirs, freirs wald never I yow assure,
That ony Prelats usit preiching:
And Prelats tuke on them that cure,
Freirs wald get nathing for thair fleiching.
Thairfoir I counsall yow fra hand,
Banische yon freir out of this land,
And that incontinent:
Do ye nocht sa withoutin weir,
He will mak all this toun on steir,
I knaw his fals intent.
Yon Priores withoutin fabill,
I think scho is nocht profitabill,
For Christis regioun.
To begin reformatioun,
Mak of them deprivatioun,
This is my opinioun.

FIRST SERGEANT: Sir pleis ye that we twa invaid them,
And ye sall se us sone degraid them,
Of coill and chaplarie?

CORRECTIOUN: Pas on Iam richt weill content.
Syne banische them incontinent
Out of this cuntrie.

FIRST SERGEANT: Cum on sir freir and be nocht fleyit,
    The King our maister mon be obeyit,
    Bot ye sall haue na harme:
    Gif ye wald travell fra toun to toun,
    I think this hude and heauie goun
    Will hald your wambe ovir warme.

FLATTERIE: Freir Now quhat is this that thir monster meins?
    I am exemptit fra Kings and Queens,
    And fra all humane law:

SECUND SERGEANT: Tak ye the hude and I the gown,
    This timmer luiks als lyke ane lown,
    As any that ever I saw.

FIRST SERGEANT: Thir freirs to chaip punitioun,
    Haulds them at their exemptioun,
    And na man will obey:
    Thay ar exempt I yow assure,
    Baith fra Paip, kyng and Empreour,
    And that maks all the pley.

SECUND SERGEANT: On Dumisday quhen Christ sall say
    Venite benedicti:

    The Freirs will say without delay
    Nos sumus exempts.

Heir sall thay spuilye Flattrie of the Freirs habite.

GUDE-COUNSELL: Sir be the halie Trinite,
    This same is feinyeit Flattrie,
    I ken him be his face:
    Beleiuand for to get promotioun,
    He said that his name was Devotioun,
    And sa be gyiit your grace,

FIRST SERGEANT: Cum on my Ladie Priores,
    We sall leir yow to dance:
    And that within ane lytill space,
    Ane new pavin of France.

Heir sall thay spuilye the Priores and scho sall haue ane kirtill of silk under hir habite.

    Now brother be the Masse,
    Be my judgement I think
    This halie Priores
    Is turnit in ane cowclink.

PRIORES: I gif my freinds my malisoun,
    That me compellit to be ane Nun

And wald nocht let me marie:
It was my freinds greadines,
That gart me be ane Priores,
Now hartlie them I warie.
Howbeit that Nunnis sing nichts and dayis,
Thair hart waitis nocht quhat thair mouth sayis
The suith I yow declair:
Makand yow intimatioun,
To Christis congregatioun,
Nunnis ar nocht necessair,
Bot I sall do the best I can,
And marie sum gude honest man,
And brew gude aill and tun:
Mariage be my opinioun,
It is better Religoun,
As to be freir or Nun.

FLATTERIE: My Lords for Gods saik let not hang me
Howbeit that widdiefows wald wrang me
I can mak na debait:
To win my meat at pleuch nor harrowis,
Bot I sall help to hang my marrowis,
Baith Falset and Dissait.

CORRECTIOUN: Than pas thy way & greath the gallous
Syne help for to hang up thy fellow is,
Thou gets na uther grace:
Of that office I am content,
Bot our Prelates I dread repent,
Be I fleimde from thair face.

Heir sall Flatterie sit besyde his marrowis.

DISSAIT: Now Flattrie my auld companyeoun,
Quhat dois yon King Correctioun?
Knawis thou nocht his intent?
Declair to us of thy novellis:
Ye'ile all be hangit, I se nocht ellis,
And that incontinent.

DISSAIT: Now walloway will ye gar hang us?
she Devill brocht yon curst king amang us,
For mekill sturt and stryfe:

FLATTERIE: I had bene put to deid amang yow,
War nocht I tuke on hand till hang yow,
And sa I saisit my lyse.
I heir them say thay will cry doun,
All freirs and Nunnis in this Regioun,
Sa far as I can feill:

Becaus thay ar nocht necessair,
And als thay think thay ar contrair,
To Johne the common-weill.

Heir sall the Kings and the Temporal stait round togider.

CORRECTIOUN: With the advice of King Humanitie,
    Heir I determine with rype advysement,
    That all thir Prelats sall deprivit be,
    And be decreit of this present Paliament,
    That thir thrie cunning Clarks sapient
    Immediatlie thair places sall posses:
    Becaus that thay haue bene sa negligent,
    Suffring the word of God for till decres.

REX: As ye haue said but dout it salbe done,
    Pas to and mak this interchainging sone.

The Kings servants lay hands on the thrie prelats & says.

WANTONNES: My Lords we pray yow to be patient,
    For we will do the Kings commandement,

SPIRITUALITIE: I mak ane vow to God and ye us handill,
    Ye sallbe curst and gragit with buik and candill:
    Syne we sall pas unto the Palp and pleinyie,
    And to the Devill of hell condemne this meinye,
    For quhy sic reformatioun as I weine
    Into Scotland was never hard nor seine.

Heir sall thay spuilye them with silence and put thair habite on the thrie Clarks.

MERCHANT: We mervell of yow paintit sepulturis.
    That was sa bauld for to accept sic cuiris.
    With glorious habit rydand upon your Muillis,
    Now men may se ye ar bot verie fuillis.

SPIRITUALITIE: We say the Kings war greiter fuillis nor we
    That us promovit to sa greit dignitie.

ABBOT: Thair is ane thowsand in the kirk but doubt,
    Sic fuillis as'we gif thay war weill socht out,
    Now brother sen it may na better be,
    Let us gasoup with Sensualitie.

Heir sall thay pas to Sensualitie.

SPIRITUALITIE: Madame I pray yow mak us thrie gude cheir,
    We cure nocht to remaine with yow all yeir.

SENSUALITIE: Pas fra us fuillis be him that hes us wrocht
    Ye ludge nocht heir, becaus I knaw yow nocht.

SPIRITUALITIE: Sir Covetice will ye also misken me?
    I wait richt weill ye wil baith gif and len me:
    Speid hand my freind spair nocht to break the lockis,
    Gif me ane thowsand crouns out of my box.

COVETICE: Quhairfoit sir fuil gif yow ane thowsand crowns –
    Ga hence ye seime to be thrie verie lowns.

SPIRITUALITIE: I se nocht els brother withoutin faill,
    Bot this fals warld is turnit top ouir taill:
    Senall is vaine that is under the lift,
    To win our meat we man make uther schift.
    With our labour except we mak debait,
    I dreid full sair we want baith drink and meat.

PERSONE: Gif with our labour we man us defend,
    Then let us gang quhair we war never kend.

SPIRITUALITIE: I wyte thir freirs that I am thus abusit,
    For by thair counsall I haue bene confusit.
    Thay gart me trow it suffysit allace,
    To gar them plainlie preich into my place.

ABBOT: Allace, this reformatioun I may warie,
    For I haue yit twa dochters for to marie –
    And thay ar baith contractit be the Rude,
    And waits nocht how to pay thair tocher-gude.

PERSONE: The Devill mak cair for this unhappie chance,
    For I am young and thinks to pas to France.
    And tak wages amang the men of weir,
    And win my living with my sword and speir.

The Bischop, Abbot, Persone, and Priores depaires altogidder.

GUDE-COUNSALL: Or ye depairt sir aff this Regioun,
    Gif Johne the Common-weill ane gay garmoun:
    Becaus the Common-weill hes bene overluikit,
    That is the caus that Common-weill is cruikit.
    With singular profeit he hes bene sa supprysit,
    That he is baith cauld, naikit and disgysit.

CORRECTIOUN: As ye haue said father I am content,
    Sergeants gif Johne ane new abuilyement.
    Of Sating, Damais or of the Velvot fyne,
    And gif him place in our Parliament syne.

Heir sall thay cleith Johne the Common-weil gorgeouslie and set him doun amang them in the Parliament.

    All verteous peopil now may be reioisit,

Sen Common-weill hes gottin ane gay garmoun:
And ignorants out of the Kirk deposit,
Devoit Doctours and Clarks of renoun
Now in the Kirk sall haue dominioun:
And Gude-counsall with Ladie Veritie
Ar profest with our kings Maiestie.
Blist is that Realme that hes ane prudent King,
Quhilk dois delyte to heir the veritie,
Punisching tha me that plainlie dois maling,
Contrair the Common-weill and equitie.
Thair may na peopill haue prosperitie,
Quhair ignorance hes the dominioun,
And common-weil be tirants trampit doun.

Pausa.

Now maisters ye sall heir incontinent,
At great leysour in your presence proclamit
The Nobill Acts of our Parliament,
Of quhilks we neid nocht for to be aschamit,
Cum heir trumpet & sound your warning tone
That every man may knaw quhat he haue done.

Heir sall Diligence with the Scrybe and the trumpet pas to the pulpit and proclame the Actis.

The First Act

It is devysit be thir prudent Kings,
Correctioun and King Humanitie,
That thair Leigis induring all thair Ringis,
With the avyce of the estaits thrie
Sall manfullie defend and fortifie
The Kirk of Christ and his Religioun,
Without dissimulance or hypocrisie:
Under the paine of thair punitioun.

Als thay will that the Acts honorabill,
Maid be our Prince in the last Parliament,
Becaus thay ar baith gude and profitabill,
Thay willl that everie man be diligent
Them till observe with vnseinyeit intent.
Quha disobey is inobedientlie
Be thair law is but doubt thay sall repent,
And painis conteinit thairin sall underly,

And als the Common-weil for til advance,
It is statute that all the Temporall lands,
Be set in few efter the forme of France
Til verteous men that labours with thair hands,
Resonabillie restrictit with sic bands,

That thay do service nevertheles
And to besubiect ay vnder the wands:
That riches may with policie incres.

Item this prudent Parliament hes devysit,
Gif Lords halds under thair dominioun
Theifis, quhair throch puir peopil bein supprisit:
For them thay sall make answeir to the croun,
And to the pure mak restitutioun:
Without thay put them in the iudges hands,
For thair default to suffer punitioun,
Sa that na theifis remaine within thair lands.

To that intent that Justice sould incres
It is concludit in this Parliament,
That into Elgin or into Innernesse
Sall be ane sute of Clarks sapient,
Togidder with ane prudent Precident
To do Justice in all the Norther Airtis,
Sa equallie without impediment,
That thay neid nocht seik Justice in thir pairts.

With licence of the Kirks halines,
That iustice may be done continuallie,
All the maters of Scotland mair and les,
To thir twa famous saits perpetuallie
Salbe directit, becaus men seis plainlie,
Thir wantoun Nunnis ar na way necessair,
Till Common-weill nor yit to the glorie
Of Christs Kirk, thocht thay be fat and fair.
And als that fragill ordour feminine,
Will nocht be missit in Christs Religioun,
Thair rents usit till ane better fyne:
For Common-weill of all this Regioun.
Ilk Senature for that erectioun,
For the uphalding of thair gravitie
Sall haue fyue hundreth mark of pensioun.
And also bot twa sall thair nummer be
Into the North saxteine sall thair remaine,
Saxtein rycht sa in our maist famous toun
Of Edinburgh to serve our Soveraine:
Chosen without partiall affectioun
Of the maist cunning Clarks of this Regioun:
Thair Chancellar chosen of ane famous Clark,
Ane cunning man of great perfectioun,
And for his pensioun haue ane thowsand mark.

It is devysit in this Parliament,
From this day furth na mater Temporall

Our new Prelats thairto hes done consent
Cum befoir judges consistoriall,
Quhilk hes bene sa prolixt and partiall:
To the great hurt of the communitie:
Let Temporall men seik judges Temporall,
And Sprituall men to Spiritualitie.

Na benefice beis giffin in tyme cumming,
Bot to men of gude eruditioun:
Expert in the halie Scripture and cunning,
And that thay be of gude conditioun:
Of publick vices but suspitioun,
And qualefiet richt prudentlie to preich,
To thair awin folk baith into land and toun
Or ellis in famous scuillis for to teich:
Als becaus of the great pluralitie
Of ignorant Preists ma then ane Legioun.
Qi hair throch of Teicheouris the heich dignitie,
Is vilipendit in ilk Regioun,
Thairfoir our Court hes maid provisioun,
That na Bshops mak teichours in tyme cumming:
Except men of gude eruditioun,
And for Preistheid qualefeit and cunning,
Siclyke as ye se in the borrows toun
Ane Tailyeour is nocht sufferit to remaine,
Without he can mak doublet, coat and gown,
He man gang till his prenteischip againe:
Bischops sould nocht ressaue me think certaine,
Into the Kirk except ane cunning Clark:
Ane idiot preist Esay compaireth plaine,
Till ane dum dogge that can nocht byte nor bark.

From this day furth se na Prelats pretend,
Under the paine of inobedience
At Prince or Paip to purchase ane command
Againe the kow becaus it dois offence:
Till ony Preist we think sufficience
And benefice for to serve God withall,
Twa Prelatssall na man haue from thence,
Without that he be of the blude Royall.

Item this prudent counsall hes concludit,
Sa that our haly Vickars be nocht wraith
From this day furth thay salbe cleane denudit
Baith of corspresent cow and umest claith.
To pure commons becaus it hath done skaith
And mairouer we think it lytill force,
Howbeit the Barrouns thairto will be laith,
From thine-furth thay sall want thair hyrald hors.

It is decreit that in this Parliament
Ilk Bischop Minister, Priour and Persoun,
To the effect thay may tak better tent
To saulis under thair dominioun,
Efter the forme of thair fundatioun,
Ilk Bischop in his Diosie sall remaine:
And everilk Persone in his parachoun,
Teiching thair folk from vices to refraine.

Becaus that clarks our substance dois consume
For bils and proces of thair prelacies:
Thairfoir thair sall na money ga to Rome
From this day furth or any benefice:
Bot gif it be for greit Archbischopries,
As for the rest na money gais at all:
For the incressing of thair dignities,
Na mair nor did to Peter nor to Paull.

Considering yat our Preists for the maist part
Thay want the gift of Chastitie wese:
Cupido hes sa perst them throch the hart,
We grant them licence and frie libertie,
That thay may haue fair Virgins to thair wyfis:
And sa keip matrimoniall Chastitie,
And nocht in huirdome for to leid thair lyfis.

This Parliament richt sa hes done conclude
From this day forth our Barrouns temporall,
Sall na mair mix thair nobil ancient blude
With bastard bairns of Stait Spirituall:
Ilk stait amang thair awin selfis marie sall,
Gif Nobils marie with the Spritualitie,
From thyne subiect thay salbe, and all
Sal be degraithit of thair Nobilitie.
And from amang the Nobils cancellit:
Unto the tyme thay by thair libertie,
Rehabilit be the ciuill magistrate
And sa sall marie the Spiritualitie.
Bichops with bischops sall mak affinitie,
Abbots and Priors with the Priores:
As Bischop Annas in Scripture we may se,
Maryit his dochter on Bischop Caiphas.
Now haue ye heard the Acts honorabill,
Devysit in this present Parliament,
To Common-weill we think agreabill:
All faithfull folk sould heirof be content,
Them till observe with hartlie trew intent,
I wait nane will against our Acts rebell,

Nor till our law be inobedient,
Bot Plutois band the potent prince of hell.

Heir sall Pauper cum befoir the King and say.

PAUPER: I gif yow my braid bennesoun,
  That hes givin Common-weill a goun:
  I wald nocht for ane pair of plackis,
  Ye had nocht maid this nobill Actis.
  I pray to God and sweit Sanct Geill,
  To gif yow grace to use them weill:
  Wer thay weill keipit I understand,
  It war great honour to Scotland.
  It had bene als gude ye had sleipit,
  As to mak acts and be nocht keipit:
  Bot I beseik yow for Alhallows,
  To heid Dissait and hang his fellows.
  And banische Flattrie aff the toun,
  For thair was never sic ane loun.
  That beand done I hauld it best,
  That everie man ga to his rest.
  Correctioun As thou hes said it salbe done,
  Suyith Sergeants hang yon swingeours sone.

Heir sall the Sergeants lous the presoners out of the and stocks leid them the to gallows.

FIRST SERGEANT: Cum heir sir Theif, cum heir, cum heir
  Quhen war ye wont to be sa sweir?
  To hunt Cattell ye war ay speidie
  Thairfoir ye sall weaue in ane widdie.

THIFT: Man I be hangit allace, allace,
  Is thair nane heir may get me grace?
  Yit or I die gif me ane drink.

FIRST SERGEANT: Fy huirsun carle I feil ane stink.

THIFT: Thocht I wald nocht that it wittin
  Sir in gude faith I am bedirtin:
  To wit the veritie gif ye pleis
  Louse doun my hois put in your neis.

FIRST SERGEANT: Thou art ane limmer I stand foird
  Slip in thy head into this coird:
  For thou had never ane meiter tippit,

THIFT: Allace this is ane fellon rippit.

Pausa.

  The widdifow wairdanis tuke my geir,
  And left me nether hors nor meir:

Nor earthlie gude that me belangit,
Now walloway I man be hangit.
Repent your lyfis, ye plaine oppressours,
All ye misdoras and transgreslours:
Or ellis gar chuse yow gude confessours,
And mak yow forde:
For gif ye tarie in this land,
And cum under Correctiouns hand:
Your grace salbe I understand,
Ane gude scharp coird.
Adew my bretheren common theifis,
That helpit me in my mischeifis.
Adew Grosars, Nicksons and Bellis
Oft haue we run out-thoart the fellis.
Adew Robsonis, Haues and Pyslilis
That in our craft hes mony wyllis.
Lytils Trumbels and Armestrangs,
Adew all theifis that me belangs·
Tailyeours, Curwings and Elwands,
Speidie of fut and wicht of hands.
The Scottis of Ewisdaill and the Graimis
I haue na tyme to tell your namis:
With King Correctioun and ye be fangit,
Beleif richt weill ye wilbe hangit.

FIRST SERGEANT: Speid hand man with thy clitter clatter.

THIFT: For Gods saik sir let me mak watter.
    Howbeit I haue bene cattel-gredie
    It schamis to pische into ane widdie.

Heir sall Thift be drwin up, or his figour.

SECUND SERGEANT: Cum heir Dissait my companyeoun
    Saw ever ane man lyker ane loun?
    To hing upon ane gallows:

DISSAIT: This is aneuch to make me mangit,
    Duill fell me, that I man be hangit,
    Let me speik with my fallows.
    I trow wan-fortune brocht me heir
    Quhat mekill feind maid me sa speidie?
    Sen it was said it is sevin yeir,
    That I sould weaue into ane widdie,
    I leirit my maisters to be gredie,
    Adew, for I se na remeid:
    Luke quhat it is to be evil-deidie.

SECUND SERGEANT: Now in this halter slip thy hand,
    Stand still, me think ye draw aback:

DISSAIT: Allace maister ye hurt my crag,

SECUND SERGEANT: It will hurt better I woid an plak,
    Richt now quhen ye hing on ane knag.

DISSAIT: Adew my maisters merchant men,
    I haue yow servit as ye ken:
    Truelie baith air and lait:
    I say to yow for conclusioun,
    I dreid ye gang to confusioun,
    Fra tyme ye want Dissait.
    I leirit yow merchants mony ane wyle,
    Upalands wyfis for to begyle,
    Upon ane markit day:
    And gar them trow your stuffe was gude,
    Quhen it was rottin be the Rude,
    And sweir it was nocht sway.
    I was ay roundand in your ear,
    And leirit yow for to ban and sweir,
    Quhat your geir cost in France:
    Howbeit the Devill ane word was trew,
    Your craft gif King Correctioun knew,
    Wald turne yow to mischance.
    I leirit yow wyllis many fauld,
    To mix the new wyne and the auid,
    That faschioun was na follie:
    To sell richt deir and by gude-chaip,
    And mix Ry-meill amang the saip,
    And Saiffrone with Oyl-dolie.
    Foryet nocht ocker I counsall yow,
    Mair then the vicker dois the kow,
    Or Lords thair doubill maill:
    Howbeit your elwand be too skant,
    Or your pound wecht thrie unces want,
    Think that bot iytiil faill.
    Adew the greit Clan Iamesone,
    The blude Royal of Clappertoun,
    I was ay to yow trew:
    Baith Andersone and Patersone,
    Above them all Thome Wflliamsone,
    My absence ye will rew.
    Thome Williamsone it Is your pairt,
    To pray for me with all your hairt,
    And think upon my warks:
    How I leirit yow ane gude lessoun,
    For to begyle in Edinburgh toun,
    The Bischop and his Clarks.
    Ye young merchants may cry allace,

For wanting of your wonted grace,
Yon curst King ye may ban:
Had I leifit bot halfe ane yeir
I sould haue leirit yow crafts perqueir,
To begyle wyfe and man.
How may ye merchants mak debait?
Fra tyme ye want your man Dissait,
For yow I mak great cair:
Without I ryse fra deid to lyfe,
I wait weill ye will never thryfe,
Farther nor the fourth air.

Heir sall Dissait be drawin up or ellis his figure.

FIRST SERGEANT: Cum heir Falset & mence the gallows,
  Ye man hing up amang your fallows,
  For your cankart conditioun:
  Monie ane trew man haue ye wragnit,
  Thairfoir but doubt ye salbe hangit,
  But mercie or remissioun.

FALSET: Allace, man I be hangit to?
  Quhat mekill Devil is this ado?
  How came I to this cummer?
  My gude maisters ye crafts men,
  Want ye Falset full weill I ken,
  Ye will all die for hunger.
  Ye men of craft may cry allace,
  Quhen ye want me ye want your grace:
  Thairfoir put into wryte:
  My lessouns that I did yow leir,
  Howbeit the commons eyne ye bleir,
  Count ye nocht that ane myte.
  Find me ane Wobster that is leill,
  Orane Walker that will nocht steill,
  Thair craftines I ken:
  Or ane Millair, that is na falt,
  That will nather steill meall nor malt,
  Hauld them for halie men.
  At our fleschers tak ye na greife,
  Thocht thay blaw leane mutton and beife,
  That thay seime fat and fair:
  Thay think that practick bot ane mow,
  Howbeit the Devill a thing it dow,
  To thame I leirit that lair.
  I leirit Tailyeours in everie toun,
  To schaip fyue quarters in ane goun,
  In Angus and in Fyfe:

To uplands Tailyeours I gaue gude leife,
To steill ane sillie stump or sleife,
Unto kittok his wyfe.
My gude maister Andro Fortoun,
Of Tailyeours that may weir the croun,
For me he will be mangit:
Tailyeour Baberage my sone and air,
I wait for me will rudlie rair,
Fra tyme he se me hangit.
The barfit Deacon Jamie Ralfe,
Quha never yit bocht kow nor calfe,
Becaus he can nocht steall:
Willie Cadyeoch will make na plead,
Howbeit his wyfe want beife and bread,
Get he gude barmie aill.
To the brousters of Cowper toun,
I leife my braidblack malesoun,
Als hardie as I may:
To make thinne aill thay think na falt,
Of mekill barme and lytill malt,
Agane the market day.
And thay can mak withoutin doubt,
Ane kynde of aill thay call Harns-out,
Wait ye how thay mak that?
Ane curtill queine ane laidlie lurdane,
Of strang wesche scho will tak ane iurdane,
And settis in the gyle-fat.
Quha drinks of that aill, man or page
It will gar all his harnis rage,
That jurdane I may rew:
It gart my heid rin hiddie giddie,
Sirs God nor I die in ane widdie,
Gif this taill be nocht trew.
Speir at the Sowtar Geordie Sillie,
Fra tyme that he had fild his bellie,
With this unhelthsum aill:
Than all the Baxters will I ban,
That mixes bread with dust and bran,
And fyne flour with beir maill.
Adew my maisters Wrichts and Maissouns,
I haue neid to leir yow few lessouns,
Ye knaw my craft perqueir:
Adew blak-Smythis and Lorimers,
Adew ye craftie Cordiners,
That sellis the schone over deir,
Gold Smythis fair-weill aboue them all,
Remember my memoriall,
With mony ane sittill cast:

To mix set ye nocht by twa preinis
Fyne Ducat gold with hard Gudlingis,
Lyke as I leirnit yow last.
Quhen I was ludgit upaland,
The Schiphirds maid with me ane band,
Richt craftelie to steill:
Than did I gif ane confirmatioun,
To all the Schiphirdis of this Natioun,
That thay sould never be leill.
And ilk ane to reser ane uther,
I knaw fals Schiphirds fyftie fidder,
War thair canteleinis kend:
How thay mak in thair conventiouns,
On montans far fra ony touns,
To let them never mend.
Amang crafts men it is ane wonder,
To find ten leill amang ane hunder
The treuth I to yow tell:
Adew I may na langer tarie,
I man pas to the King of Farie,
Or ellis the rycht to hell.

Heir sall he luke up to his fallows hingand.

Wais me for the gude common thift,
Was never man maid ane mair honest schift,
His leifing for to win:
Thair was nocht ane in all Lidsdaill,
That ky mair crastelie culd staill,
Quhair thou hings on that pin.
Sathan ressaue thy saull Dissait,
Thou was to me ane faithfull mait,
Andals my father brother:
Duill fell the sillie merchant men,
To mak them service weill I ken,
Thaill never get sic ane uther.

Heir sall thay festin the coard to his neck with ane dum countenance thairefter he sall say.

Gif any man list for to be my mait,
Cum follow me for I am at the gait:
Cum follow me all catyfe covetous Kings,
Reauers but richt of uthers Realmis and Rings.
Togidder with all wrangous conquerours.
And bring with yow all publick oppressours.
With Pharao King of Egiptians
With him in hell salbe your recompence.
All cruell schedders of blude innocent,

Cum follow me or ellis rin and repent,
Prelats that hes ma benefeits nor thrie,
And will nocht teich nor preiche the veritie,
Without at God in tyme thay cry for grace,
In hiddeous hell I sall prepair thair place.
Cum follow me all fals corruptit judges,
With Pontius Pilat I sall prepair your judges
All ye officials that parts men with thair wyfis,
Cum follow me or els gang mend your lyfis:
With all fals leiders of the constrie law,
With wanton Scribs and Clarks intill ane raw.
That to the puir maks mony partiall traine,
Syne hodie ad octo bids them cum againe.
And ye that taks rewairds at baith the hands,
Ye sall with me be bund in Baliels bands.
Cum follow me all curst unhappie wyfis,
That with your gudemen dayly flytis and stryfis,
And quyetlie with rybalds makes repair,
And taks na cure to make ane wrangous air.
Ye sal in hel rewairdit be I wein,
With Iesabell of Israell the Queene.
I haue ane curst unhappie wyfe my sell,
Wald God scho war befoir me into hell:
That Bismair war scho thair withoutin doubt,
Out of hell the Devill scho wald ding out.
Ye maryit men evin as ye luife your lyfis,
Let never preists be hamelie with your wyfis.
My wyfe with preists sho doith me greit onricht
And maid me nine tymes cuckald on ane nicht.
Fairweil for I am to the widdie wend,
For quhy falset maid never ane better end.

Heir sall he be heisit up, and not his figure and an Craw or ane Ke salbe castin up as it war his saull.

FLATTERIE: Haue I nocht chaipit the widdie weil?
    Yea that I haue haue be sweit Sanct Geill,
    For I had nocht bene wrangit:
    Becaus I servit be Alhallows,
    Till haue bene merchellit amang my fellowis:
    And heich aboue them hangit.
    I maid far ma falts nor my maits,
    I begylde all the thrie estaits,
    With my hypocrisie:
    Quhen I had on my freirs hude
    All men beleifit that I was gude,
    Now judge ye gif I be.
    Tak mean rackles rubyatour,

Ane theif ane tyrane or ane tratour,
Of everie vyce the plant.
Gif him the habite of ane freir,
The wyfis will trow withoutin weir,
He be ane verie Saint.
I knaw that cowle ane skaplarie,
Genners mair hait nor charitie,
Thocht thay be blak or blew:
Quhat halines is thair within,
Ane wolfe cled in ane wedders skin,
Judge ye gif this be trew.
Sen I haue chaipit this firie farie,
Adew I will na Langer tarie,
To cumber yow with my clatter:
Bot I will with ane humbill spreit,
Gang serve the Hermeit of Lareit:
And leir him for till flatter.

Heir sall enter Foly.

FOLY: Gude day my Lords and als God saine,
Dois na man bid gude day againe?
Quhen fuillis ar fow then ar thay faine,
Ken ye nocht me?
How call thay me can ye nocht tell?
Now be him that herryit hell,
I wait nocht how thay call my sell,
Bot gif I lie.

DILIGENCE: Quhat brybour is this that maks sic beiris?

FOLY: The feind ressaue that mouth that speirs:
Gude-man ga play yow with your feiris,
With muck upon your mow:

DILIGENCE: Fond fuill quhair hes thou bene sa lait?

FOLY: Marie cummand throw the Schogait.
Bot thair hes bene ane great debait,
Betwixt me and ane Sow.
The Sow cryit guff and I to ga,
Throw speid of fute I gat awa,
Bot in the midst of the cawsa,
I fell into ane midding:
Scho lap upon me with ane bend,
Quha ever the midings sould amend,
God send them ane mischevous end,
For that is bot Gods bidding.
As I was pudlit thair God wait,
Bot with my club I maid debait:

Ise never cum againe that gait,
I sweir yow be Alhallows
I wald the officiars of the toun,
That suffers sic confusion,
That thay war harbreit with Mahown,
Or hangit on ane gallows.
Fy fy that sic ane fair cuntrie,
Sould stand sa lang but policie:
I gif them to the Devill hartlie.
That hes the wyte:
I wald the Provost wald tak in heid,
Of yon midding to make remeid,
Quhilk pat me and the Sow at feid,
Quhat may I do bot flyte?

REX: Pas on my servant Diligence,
    And bring yon suill to our presence.

DILIGENCE: That sall be done but tarying,
    Foly ye man ga to the King.

FOLY: The King, quhat kynde of thing is that?
    Is yon he with the goldin Hat?

DILIGENCE: Yon same is he, cum on thy way:

FOLY: Gif ye be King God yow gude day,
    I haue ane plaint to make to yow:

REX: Quhom on Folie? –

FOLY: Marie on ane Sow.
    Sir scho hes sworne that scho sall sla me,
    Or ellis byte baith my balloks fra me:
    Gif ye be King be Sanct Allan,
    Ye sould do justice to ilk man.
    Had I nocht keipit me with my club,
    The Sow had drawin me in ane dub.
    I heir them say thair is cum to the toun,
    Ane King callit Correctioun.
    I pray, yow tell me quhilk is he:

DILIGENCE: Yon with the wings, may hocht se?

FOLY: Now wallie fall that weill fairde mow,
    Sir I pray yow correct yon Sow:
    Quhilk with hir teith but sword or knyfe,
    Had maist haue reft me of my lyfe:
    Gif ye will nocht mak correctioun,
    Than gif me your protectioun
    Of all Swyne for to be skaithles
    Betuix this toun and Innernes.

190

DILIGENCE: Foly hes thou ane wyfe at hame?

FOLY: Yea that I haue, God send hir schame:
    Itrow be this scho is neir deid,
    I left ane wyfe bind and hir heid,
    To schaw hir seiknes I think schame,
    Scho hes sic rumbling in hir wambe:
    That all the nicht my hart overcasts,
    With bocking and with thunder-blasts,

DILIGENCE: Peradventure scho be with bairne:

FOLY: Allace I trow scho be forfairne.
    Scho sobbit and scho feil in sown,
    And than thay rubbit hir up and doun:
    Scho riftit, routit and maid sic stends,
    Scho yeild and gaid at baith the ends.
    Till scho had castin ane cuppill of quarts
    Syne all turn it to ane rickill of farts.
    Scho blubert, bockit and braik it still,
    Hir arsse gaid evin lyke ane wind mill.
    Scho stumblit and stutterit with sic stends,
    That scho recanti at baith the ends.
    Sik dismell drogs fra hir scho schot,
    Quhill scho maid all the fluir on flot.
    Of hir hurdies scho scho had na hauld,
    Quhill scho had twmed hir monyfauld:

DILIGENCE: Better bring hir to the Leitches heir:

FOLY: Trittill trattill, scho may nocht steir,
    Hir verie buttoks maks sic beir,
    It skars baith foill and fillie:
    Scho bocks sik bagage fra hir breist,
    He wants na bubbils that sittis hir neist,
    And ay scho cryis a preist a preist,
    With ilk a quhillie lillie.

DILIGENCE: Recoverit scho nocht at the last?

FOLY: Yea bot wit ye weil scho fartit fast.
    Bot quhen scho sichis my hart is sorie,

DILIGENCE: Bot drinks scho ocht?

FOLY: Ye be Sanct Marie,
    Ane quart at anis it will nocht tarie,
    And leif the Devill a drap:
    Than sic flobbage scho layis fra hir,
    About the wallis, God wait sic wair,

Quhen it was drunkin I gat to skair,
The lickings of the cap.

DILIGENCE: quhat is in that creill I pray the tell?

FOLY: Marie I haue Folie Hats to sell.

DILIGENCE: I pray the sell me ane or tway:
Folie Na tarie quhill the market day,
I will sit doun heir be Sanct Clune,
And gif my babies thair disiune.
Cum heir gude Glaiks my dochter deir
Thousalbe maryit within ane yeir,
Upon ane freir of Tillilum,
Na thou art nather deaf nor dum:
Cum hidder Stult my sone and air,
My joy thou art baith gude and fair:
Now sall I efnd yow as I may
Thocht ye cry lyke ane Ke all day.

Heir sall the bairns cry keck lyke ane Kae and he sal put meat in thair mouth.

DILIGENCE: Get up Folie but tarying,
And speid yow haistelie to the King
Get up me think the carle is dum.

FOLY: Now bum baleriebum bum.

DILIGENCE: I trow the trucour lyis in ane trance
Get up man with ane mirrie mischance:
Or be Sanct Dyonis of France,
Ise gar the want thy wallet:
Its schame to se man how thow lyis,

FOLY: Wa yit againe now this is thryis:
The Devill wirrie me and I ryse,
Bot I sall break thy pallet.
Me think my pillok will nocht ly doun,
Hauld doun your head ye lurdon loun,
Yon fair las with the Sating goun
Gars yow thus bek and bend:
Take thair ane neidill for your cace
Now for all the hiding of your face,
Had I yow in ane quyet place.
Ye wald nocht waine to fiend.
Thir bony armis that ar cled in silk,
Ar evin als wantoun as any wilk,
I wald forbeir baith bread and milk
To kis thy bony lippis:
Suppois ye luke as ye war wraith,
War ye at quyet behind ane claith,

    Ye wald not stick to preife my graith,
    With hobling of your hippis.

DILIGENCE: Suyith harlot haist the to the King
    And let allane thy trattilling.
    Lo heir is Folie sir alreadie,
    Ane richt sweir swingeour be our Ladie.

FOLY: Thou art not half sa sweir thy sell,
    Quhat meins this pulpit, I pray the tell?

DILIGENCE: Our new Bischops hes maid ane preiching,
    Bot thou heard never sic pleasant teiching:
    Yon Bischop will preich throch the coast,

FOLY: Than stryk ane hag into the poast,
    For I hard never in all my lyfe,
    Ane Bischop cum to preich in Fyfe.
    Gif Bischops to be preichours leiris,
    Wallaway quhat sall word of freiris?
    Gif Prelats preich in brugh and land,
    The sillie freirs I understand
    Thay will get na mair meall nor malt,
    Sa I dreid freirs sall die for falt.
    Sen sa is that yon nobill King,
    Will mak men Bischops for preiching:
    Quhat say ye sirs, hauld ye nocht best?
    That I gang preich amang the rest.
    Quhen I haue preichit on my best wayis,
    Then will I sell my merchandise,
    To my bretherin and tender maits,
    That dwels amang the thrie estaits.
    For I haue heir gude chaifery,
    Till any fuill that lists to by.

Heir sall Foly hing up his hattis on the pulpet and say.

    God sen I had ane Doctours hude.

REX: Quhy Folie wald thou mak ane preiching?

FOLY: Yea that I wald sir be the Rude,
    But eyther flattering or fleiching.

REX: Now brother let us heir his teiching,
    To pas our tyme and heir him raise.

DILIGENCE: He war far meiter for the kitching,
    Amang the pottis sa Christ me saife.
    Fond Foly sall I be thy Clark,
    And answeir the ay with amen:

FOLY: Now at the beginning of my wark,
    The feind ressaue that graceles grim.

Heir sall Foly begin hir sermon, as followis.

Stultorum numerus infinitus.

Salomon the maist sapient King
In Israell quhan he did ring,
Thir words in effect did write,
The number of fuillis ar infinite.
I think na schame sa Christ me saife,
To be ane fuill amang the laife,
Howbeit ane hundreth stands heir by,
Preventure als great fuillis as I.
Stultorum.

I haue of my Genelogie,
Dwelland in everie cuntrie,
Earles, Duiks, Kings, and Empriours,
With mony guckit Conquerours:
Quhilk dois in Folie perseveir,
And hes done sa this many yeir.
Sum seiks to warldlie dignities,
And sum to sensuall vanities
Quhat vails all thir vaine honours,
Nocht being sure to leife twa houris?
Sum greidie fuill dois fill ane box,
Ane uther fuill cummis and breaks the lox:
And spends that uther fuillis hes spaird,
Quhilk never thocht on them to wairde.
Sum dois as thay sould never die,
Is nocht this folie, quhat say ye?
Sapientia huius mundi stultitia est apud Deum.

Becaus thair is sa many fuillis,
Rydand on hors and sum on muillis:
Heir I haue bocht gude chafery,
Till ony fuill that lists to by.
And speciallie for the thrie estaits,
Quhair I haue mony tender maits:
Quhilk causit them as ye may se,
Gang backwart throw the haill cuntrie.
Gif with my merchandise ye list to mell,
Heir I haue Folie Hattis to sell.
Quhairfoir is this Hat wald ye ken?
Marie for insatiabill merchant men.
Quhen God hes send them abundance
Ar nocht content with sufficiance.
Bot saillis into the stormy blastis,

In Winter to get greater castis:
In mony terribill great torment,
Against the Acts of Parliament.
Sum tynis thair geir, and sum ar drounde,
With this sic merchants sould be crounde.

DILIGENCE: Quhom to schaips thou to sell that hude?
I trow to sum great man of gude.

FOLY: This hude to sell richt faine I wald,
Till him that is baith auld & cald:
Reddie till pas to hell or heavin,
And hes fair bairns sax or seavin:
And is of age fourscoir of yeir,
And taks ane lasse to be his peir:
Quhilk is nocht fourteine yeir of age,
And joynis with hir in mariage:
Geifand hir traist that scho nocht wald,
Rycht haistelie mak him cuckald,
Quha maryes beand sa neir thair dead,
Set on this Hat upon his head.

DILIGENCE: Quhat Hude is that tell me I pray the?

FOLY: This is ane haly Hude I say the,
This Hude is ordanit I the assure,
For Sprituall fuillis that taks in cure,
The saullis of great Diosies,
And regiment of great Abesies,
For gredines of warldlie pelfe,
Than can nocht justlie gyde them selfe.
Uthers sauls to saife it settis them weill,
Syne sell them a win saullis to the Deuil.
Quha ever dois sa, this I conclude,
Upon his heid set on this Hude:
Diligence, Foly is thair ony sic men
Now in the Kirk that thou can ken?
How sall I ken them? —

FOLY: Na keip that clois,
Ex operibus eorum cognoscetis eos.
And fuillis speik of the Prelacie,
It will be hauldin for herisie.

REX: Speik on hardlie I gif the leife:

FOLY: Than my remissioun is in my sleife.
Will ye leife me to speik of Kings?

REX: Yea hardlie speik of all kin things.

Conforming to my first narratioun,
Ye ar all fuillis be Coks passioun.

DILIGENCE: Thou leis, I trow thisfuill be man git.

FOLY: Gif I lie God nor thou behangit.
For I haue heir I to the tell
Ane nobill cap imperiell,
Quhilk is nocht ordanit bot for doings,
Of Empreours, of Duiks and Kings.
For princelie and imperiall fuillis,
Thay sould haue luggis als lang as Muillis.
The pryde of Princes without in faill,
Gars all the warld rin top ovir taill.
To win them warldlie gloir and gude,
Thay cure nocht schedding of saikles blude.
Quhat cummer haue ye had in Scotland,
Be our auld enemies of Ingland?
Had nocht bene the support of France,
We had bene brocht to great mischance.
Now I heir tell the Empreour,
Schaippis for till be ane Conquerour.
And is muifing his ordinance,
Against the Nobill King of France.
Bot I knaw nocht his just querrell,
That he hes for till mak battell.
All the Princes of Almanie,
Spainye, Flanders and Italie.
This present yeir ar in ane flocht:
Sum sall thair wages find deir bocht.
The Paip with bombard, speir and scheild,
Hes send his armie to the feild.
Sanct Peter, Sanct Paull nor Sanct Androw,
Raisit never sic ane Oist I trow.
Is this fraternall charitie,
Or furious folie, quhat say ye?
Thay leird nocht this at Christis Scuillis:
Thairfoir I think them verie fuillis.
I think it folie be Gods mother,
Ilk Christian Prince to ding doun uther:
Becaus that this hat sould belang them,
Gang thou and part it evin amang them,
The Prophesie withouttin weir,
Of Merling beis compleit this yeir:
For my gudame the Gyre Carling,
Leirnde me the Prophesie of Marling:
Quhairof I sall schaw the sentence,
Gif ye will gif me audience.

Flan Fran resurgent, simul Hispan viribus urgent,
Dani vastabunt, Vallones valla parabunt.
Sic tibi nomen in a mulier cacauit in olla:
Hoc epulum comedes −

DILIGENCE: Marie that is ane il sauorit dische.

FOLY: Sa be this Prophesie plainlie appeirs,
That mortall weirs salbe amang freirs:
Thay sall nocht knaw weill in thair closters.
To quhom thay sall say thair Pater nosters.
Wald thay fall to and fecht with speir and sheild
The feind mak cuir quhilk of them win the feild.
Now of my sermon haue I maid ane end,
To Gilly-mouband I yow all commend.
And I yow all beseik richt hartfullie:
Pray for the saull of gude Cacaphatie:
Quhilk laitlic drownit himself into Loch leavin,
That his sweit saull may be aboue the heavin.

DILIGENCE: Famous peopil hartlie I yow requyre,
This lytill sport to tak in patience,
We traist to God and we leif ane uther yeir,
Quhair we haue failit we sall do diligence,
With mair pleasure to mak yow recompence:
Becaus we haue bene sum part tedious
With mater rude, denude of eloquence,
Likewyse perchance, to sum men odious.

Now let ilk man his way avance,
Let sum ga drink and sum ga dance:
Menstrell, blaw up ane brawll of France,
Let se quha hobbils best:
For I will rin incontinent,
To the Tavern or ever I stent:
And pray to God omnipotent,
To send yow all gude rest.

The End of Ane Satyre of the Thrie Estates

Note on the Text

Any Satyre of the Thrie Estaites is a morality play in Middle Scots, first performed in June 1552 in Cuper, Fife and then in Edinburgh in 1554: both performances were outdoors. There are different manuscript versions of the text. The spelling is erratic but generally the following letters used have a modern equivalent, namely:

qu = w
i = j or i
s = sh or s
f = f or v
v = u or v
u = v or u
o = e or o
be = by

Glossary

banes	curse	graith	prepare
blade	jaw	grice	pig
bostous	rough		
brocks	badgers	halse	neck
bummill baty	booby	harne-pan	bald head
cavell	low fellow	ingyne	ability
cleikit	caught		
consuetude	custom	kow-clink	prostitute
corpse-present	death due		
couthers	gamblers	laif	rest
coy	quiet	leiris	learns
cude	christening gown	lift	sky
cummer	friend	limmer	rascal
craig	neck	lufe	palm
		lychtlyit	made light of
dang	beat		
dryte	deficate	mane	mean
		mangit	confounded
fence	proclaim	menyie	pack
ferlie	wonder	mowis	commonplace
fleyd	scared	murmell	unrest
forfair	endure		
fray	fear	nowt	cattle
glaiks	deception	oversile	obscure
graip	grasp	oyl-dolie	olive oil

Pace	Easter
paiks	punishment
perqueir	by heart
playfeir	mate
preife	try
quintessencers	alchemists
rapploch	course cloth
Roy	King
sain	bless
saip	soap
Sanct	Saint
shent	lost
siccar	sure
sleepand	sleeping
smored	smothered
steir	uproar
sowtar	shoemaker
suith	truth
sweir	unwilling
swingeours	idle rogues
swyfe	have sex
thoill	suffer
turnes	empties
verament	truth
wait	know
wary	curse
weir	doubt
widdiefows	rascals
widdy	noose